W9-BAE-188

HOW DEMOCRACY WILL ELECT THE ANTICHRIST

Virtually all Scripture references are quoted from the King James translation of the Holy Bible. The German translation of Dr. Martin Luther and the JPS translation of the Hebrew text for the Old Testament have also been used for further clarity.

How Democracy Will Elect the Antichrist

West Columbia, South Carolina 29170
Published by The Olive Press, a division of Midnight Call Ministries
West Columbia, SC 29170 U.S.A.

Copy Typist:	Lynn Jeffcoat
Copy Editor:	Susanna Cancassi
Layout/Design:	Michelle Kim
Lithography:	Simon Froese
Cover Design:	Michelle Kim

Library of Congress Cataloging-in-Publication Data

Froese, Arno
How Democracy Will Elect the Antichrist
ISBN #978-0-937422-64-9

1. Bible—Prophecy—Israel—Democracy 2. Antichrist

Printed in the United States of America

The sole purpose of publishing this book is to encourage the readers to surrender and consecrate their lives to Christ.

All funds received from the sale of this book will be used exclusively for the furtherance of the Gospel.

No one associated with this ministry receives a royalty for any of the literature published by Midnight Call Ministries, Inc.

CONTENTS

A NOTE FROM THE AUTHOR

The world today is ruled by some form of democracy. So, if this form of government were so popular, then why would I have selected such a controversial title for this book?

Winston Churchill said it best: "Democracy is the worst form of government, but it is the best we have." In this book we will focus our concern about democracy relating to prophecy — past, present and future.

Although the origin of democracy can be traced back as far as 500 B.C., true democracy — for the people and by the people — began with the Industrial Revolution. Today there is no alternative to democracy, thus many people believe that democracy is the best remedy for most of today's societal ills. Global democracy has become a decisive force for the entire world, particularly since the fall of the Soviet Union.

The Bible makes it clear that there will be unity in the end stages of the endtimes, and the world will be led by one who is loved and adored: "And I saw one of his heads as it were wounded to death; and his deadly wound was healed: and all the world wondered after the beast. And they worshipped the dragon which gave power unto the beast: and they worshipped the beast, saying, Who is like unto the beast? who is able to make war with him?"(Revelation 13:3-4). Such unity is unprecedented, but will be brought about by demonic deception. The creation of a global society, led by a supreme ruler, will not happen by force but people will gladly support this new, free and prosperous world society, thus, democracy *will* elect the Antichrist.

This updated and expanded edition of *How Democracy Will Elect the Antichrist* is a helpful resource that reveals the progression of global civilization and its desired goal for peace and safety. But Bible prophecy predicts quite the opposite: "For when they shall say, Peace and safety; then sudden destruction cometh upon them, as travail upon a woman with child; and they shall not escape" (1Thessalonians 5:3).

CHAPTER 1

WHY STUDY THE FUTURE?

Almost one-third of Holy Scripture contains a prophetic element; therefore, it is important for us to study future events. This chapter reveals why true believers in Jesus Christ are waiting for His return. It also clarifies fundamental differences between believing the prophetic Word with our mind and believing it with our heart.

Why Study the Future?

People often ask me why we should study the future. I usually give the following three answers:

First, God invites us to: "Thus saith the Lord, the Holy One of Israel, and his Maker, Ask me of things to come concerning my sons, and concerning the work of my hands command ye me" (Isaiah 45:11). God is confirming that it is good for us to ask Him about the future.

Second, the New Testament testifies: "The Revelation of Jesus Christ, which God gave unto him, to shew unto his servants things which must shortly come to pass; and he sent and signified it by his angel unto his servant John" (Revelation 1:1). Thus, God's intention for us is to know the future.

Third, our human nature wants to know as much about the future as possible so that we can better prepare for it.

Most radio stations broadcast an hourly weather forecast. Newspapers provide the reader with a complete forecast based on developing weather patterns. We consult the newspaper, watch the news and listen to the radio to see if the weather will cooperate with the outdoor activities we have planned for the following week.

Most people consult a map when they take a trip. At the very least, we want to know the distance we will have to travel to get from Point A to Point B. Some people will even research what they can expect to see when they arrive at their final destination.

A great deal of planning must be done when we travel to another country. Let's assume we're planning a trip to Israel. In order to be properly prepared for our journey we will need to find out our departure and arrival times, whether we need a visa or a passport, weather conditions, languages that are spoken, accepted currency, and if the electrical power is compatible with our blow dryers and electric shavers. These and hundreds of other questions will continue to crop up as we draw closer to the date of our departure.

Whenever we come across a book or an article in a magazine about our destination, we will read all about it. Our eyes will scan the pictures and the itinerary on our travel brochure to make sure we have not missed any details. If a program comes on television about the land of Israel, we will probably make it a top priority to watch it because we want to know what to expect when we get there.

The Importance of Preparation and Planning

I once read an article that described the preparation that was involved in the Apollo moon mission and the final goal of landing a man on the moon. The article stated that more than 500,000 engineers and technicians, representing about 20,000 corporations and firms, had participated in the Apollo mission. It took 25 years to prepare for this undertaking and cost over $25 billion! The result? In addition to man's successful landing on the moon, more than 900 pounds of moon rocks were collected for research. This mammoth project was heralded as the greatest undertaking in human history, but it was also the result of planning for the future.

Waiting for the Future

We all live for the future. Our little ones can't wait to go to school. School-aged kids want to "grow up" and go to high school. For most, the next phase of life is usually college or marriage. Each day we work, we study; we yearn for the future — for tomorrow or for next year — eagerly expecting great things for our family and ourselves.

Of course, planning for the future does not stop when people get married and have children: buying a house becomes another important goal for many. When most of our goals have been reached, or the years have caught up with us, we start preparing for retirement. We still look to the future even once we have reached retirement age — we hope to live long enough to enjoy our grandchildren and the fruit of our many years of labor.

The Future is also the End

But what happens next? Our ultimate reality is revealed in Hebrews 9:27: "It is appointed unto men once to die, but after this the judgment." Only those who have made proper preparations for the future of this reality are truly wise.

There is another reason to study the future: the future continues for eternity!

Do you now understand how important it is to study the future? It is by knowing our ultimate destiny that we can be sure of where we will spend eternity. Today is the day to make the necessary preparations for the future. Will your future be an eternity in the presence of the Savior, or will it be an eternity of suffering and damnation? The choice is yours. The Lord Jesus spoke this parable in Matthew 13:38-43 to show the obvious difference between the two:

> The field is the world; the good seed are the children of the kingdom; but the tares are the children of the wicked one; the enemy that sowed them is the devil; the harvest is the end of the world; and the reapers are the angels. As therefore the tares are gathered and burned in the fire; so shall it be in the end of this world. The Son of man shall send forth his angels, and they shall gather out of his kingdom all things that offend, and them which do iniquity; and shall cast them into a furnace of fire: there shall be wailing and gnashing of teeth. Then shall the righteous shine forth as the sun in the kingdom of their Father. Who hath ears to hear, let him hear.

To which group do you belong? We read more about these two groups of people in the book of Revelation. One group is told to rejoice while the other is given a warning: "Therefore rejoice, ye heavens, and ye that dwell in them. Woe to the inhabiters of the earth and of the sea! for the devil is come down unto you, having great wrath, because he knoweth that he hath but a short time" (Revelation 12:12).

It is significant to note here that Satan knows he has only a short time. In other words, even Satan knows about the future — he knows the Word of God, and he knows the prophetic Word; therefore, he also knows the general timing of its fulfillment.

The Devil Knows Prophecy

Matthew records the instance when two demon-possessed men approached Jesus. It is important to understand that where Jesus is, there is always truth and light, thus, darkness is immediately exposed in His presence. Jesus did not have to identify Himself to the devils, nor was it necessary for Him to do anything special. The demons exposed themselves, as we read in Matthew 8:29: "They cried out, saying, What have we to do with thee, Jesus, thou Son of God? art thou come hither to torment us before the time?"

Why did the demons protest? Because they recognized Jesus as the Son of God and Savior of the world! Apparently they knew the prophetic Word. They lamented in the form of a question: "Art thou come hither to torment us before the time?" Thus, the demons knew that Jesus would come and destroy the powers of darkness. They were aware that they would ultimately wind up in the bottomless pit, but they also knew that the time had not yet come for that to happen, which is why they asked that question!

The Bottomless Pit

Satan will be arrested and placed in confinement for a thousand years when Jesus returns to earth in great power and glory. Where will he be confined? In the bottomless pit!

> And I saw an angel come down from heaven, having the key of the bottomless pit and a great chain in his hand. And he laid hold on the dragon, that old serpent, which is the Devil, and Satan, and bound him a thousand years, and cast him into the bottomless pit, and shut him up, and set a seal upon him, that he should deceive the nations no more, till the thousand years should be fulfilled: and after that he must be loosed a little season (Revelation 20:1-3).

The bottomless pit, however, is not Satan's final destination, nor is it for those whose names are not found in the Book of Life. Their eternal destination is a much more horrible place known in Scripture as the lake of fire.

The Lake of Fire

Revelation 20:10, 12-15 describes the ultimate destination of all those who have refused salvation in Jesus Christ:

> And the devil that deceived them was cast into the lake of fire and brimstone, where the beast and the false prophet are, and shall be tormented day and night for ever and ever. And I saw the dead, small and great, stand before God; and the books were opened: and another book was opened, which is the book of life: and the dead were judged out of those things which were written in the books, according to their works. And the sea gave up the dead which were in it; and death and hell delivered up the dead which were in them: and they were judged every man according to their works. And death and hell were cast into the lake of fire. This is the second death. And whosoever was not found written in the book of life was cast into the lake of fire (Revelation 20:10, 12-15).

This passage of Scripture should be reason enough to study the future!

Spirit of Prophecy

Why study the future? Because the future is prophecy! In Revelation 19:10 we read, "For the testimony of Jesus is the spirit of prophecy." Did you know that more than a quarter of the Bible is prophetic? That's an awful lot, and it should motivate us to study the future. After all, the prophetic Word is an inseparable part of Scripture. The Bible is the only book that is truly prophetic in content. The Bible contains accounts that are past, present and future: "Behold, the former things are come to pass, and new things do I declare: before they spring forth I tell you of them" (Isaiah 42:9).

The eternal God of Israel testifies: "Ye are my witnesses, saith the LORD, and my servant whom I have chosen: that ye may know and believe me, and understand that I am he: before me there was no God formed, neither shall there be after me" (Isaiah 43:10).

Fulfilled Prophecy

The New Testament begins with a record of Bible prophecy fulfillment. Matthew 1:22 states: "that it might be fulfilled which was spoken of the Lord by the prophet." Matthew 2:15 reads: "that it might be fulfilled which was spoken of the Lord by the prophet, saying, Out of Egypt have I called my son." Verse 17 states: "Then was fulfilled that which was spoken by Jeremy the prophet." And verse 23 reads: "that it might be fulfilled which was spoken by the prophets."

The New Testament repeatedly states that Jesus is the fulfillment of Old Testament prophecies; therefore, if He is the fulfillment as written in the past, and He is the Savior today, then He must also be the fulfillment of future prophecies!

When we study the future, we are really occupying ourselves with the knowledge of our Lord Jesus Christ. After Jesus told the disciples about the events to come, He emphasized, "Behold, I have told you before" (Matthew 24:25). Jesus said, "And now I have told you before it come to pass, that, when it is come to pass, ye might believe" (John 14:29).

Fulfilled Prophecy Not Believed?

We have seen that the Bible establishes the importance of fulfilled prophecy, but we must also point out that fulfilled prophecy was not always believed.

The Jews did not believe in Jesus, nor did they believe in the fulfillment of the prophetic Word at that time, therefore, they ultimately exclaimed, "We have no king but Caesar!" This was blatant unbelief! Why didn't they believe? They relied on their preconceived ideas that the Messiah would be a military revolutionary who would liberate them from Roman occupation. From that perspective, we can understand why they did not accept Jesus as the Messiah. Of course, this rejection of Jesus was also fulfillment of Bible prophecy: "He is despised and rejected of men…and we esteemed him not" (Isaiah 53:3).

The Disciples Did Not Believe

Jesus' own disciples were among those who did not believe. When the fulfillment came to pass, and Jesus arose from the grave, we read, "And they, when they had heard that he was alive, and had been seen of her, believed not…And they went and told it unto the residue: neither believed they them." Why didn't they believe? Because they were not yet born again of the Spirit of God!

Do you recall Jesus' words to Nicodemus? He said, "Verily, verily, I say unto thee, Except a man be born again, he cannot see the kingdom of God" (John 3:3).

When our spiritual eyes are open, we will see the kingdom of God and we will study the future. We will study prophecy and we will want to know more about Jesus because He is the future!

Head or Heart Knowledge?

It is not enough to have head knowledge of the prophetic Word. We read in Matthew 2 that certain wise men from the East came to Jerusalem and asked, "Where is he that is born King of the Jews?" In verse 3 we learn that, "When Herod the king had heard these things, he was troubled, and all Jerusalem with him." Why was everyone so troubled? After all, it was a fulfillment of Old Testament prophecy!

Let me explain. We must remember that these strangers traveled to Jerusalem, the very place God had chosen as the dwelling place for His Name. Jerusalem was the center of God's plan, the center of all knowledge, and the center of direct contact with the Creator of heaven and earth.

Gentiles Acknowledge the God of Israel

More than 500 years before Jesus was born, a Gentile king named Cyrus of Persia made this profound statement when he addressed the Jews while they were in his captivity: "Who is there among you of all his people? his God be with him, and let him go up to Jerusalem, which is in Judah, and build the house of the LORD God of Israel, (he is the God,) which is in Jerusalem" (Ezra 1:3). Knowledge of God's existence was already a recorded fact.

Nebuchadnezzar, the first Gentile world ruler, made the following statement after Daniel, the Jewish prophet, had interpreted the king's dream: "Of a truth it is, that your God is a God of gods, and a Lord of kings" (Daniel 2:47).

Later, we learn that this same king established a law regarding the God of Israel after Daniel's three friends were saved from the fiery furnace: "Therefore I make a decree, That every people, nation, and language, which speak any thing amiss against the God of Shadrach, Meshach, and Abednego, shall be cut in pieces, and their houses shall be made a dunghill: because there is no other God that can deliver after this sort" (Daniel 3:29). Thus we see that the Jews and Gentiles knew about the true God.

Gentiles Announce the Birth of Christ

The wise men from the East traveled to Jerusalem in search of the newborn King. They were in the right place, they asked the right people the right questions, but they did not receive an answer right away.

First, the king closely questioned his advisers — the scribes, the intellectuals, and the religious experts of his day: "And when he had gathered all the chief priests and scribes of the people together, he demanded of them where Christ should be born" (Matthew 2:4). What was the answer? "They said unto him, In Bethlehem of Judaea: for thus it is written by the prophet" (verse 5). What a stunning statement! These Bible scholars knew where the Messiah would be born. They consulted the right source; namely, the prophetic Word, "for thus it is written by the prophet."

Now here comes the important question: Did these people in Jerusalem believe the prophetic Word? We can answer this question both yes and no. The people took the Word of God seriously enough to read and study what was written, and to base their conclusion on the prophetic Scripture that the Messiah would be born in Bethlehem. However, they only had an intellectual knowledge of the prophecies of the coming Messiah; they did not have the faith they needed in their hearts to believe. If they had believed with their hearts, then they certainly would have followed the wise men to Bethlehem and worship the newborn King. That, however, was not the case; therefore, we can rightly conclude that these people had only head knowledge of the Scriptures.

What a tragedy! They lived to see the greatest fulfillment of Bible prophecy — the birth of the Messiah — but they did not recognize it! They knew that the prophets had written about the coming One who would do mighty deeds but they chose not to see the fulfillment of Bible prophecy. They weren't really interested in studying the future or understanding the signs of the times. They were blind to the fact that

God was doing a great work in their midst! This ignorance regarding Jesus continued in Israel and it exists to this day!

Two Who Waited for Jesus

Were crowds of people waiting for Jesus when He went to the temple in Jerusalem with His parents? Only two people are mentioned who were waiting for Jesus to come at that moment! First, "And, behold, there was a man in Jerusalem, whose name was Simeon; and the same man was just and devout, waiting for the consolation of Israel: and the Holy Ghost was upon him" (Luke 2:25). That's all — there was a man. What was so special about this man that he alone is mentioned here? He was "waiting for the consolation of Israel." Are you waiting for Jesus today?

One other person is mentioned: "And there was one Anna, a prophetess, the daughter of Phanuel, of the tribe of Aser" (Luke 2:36). Anna recognized the Messiah: "And she coming in that instant gave thanks likewise unto the Lord, and spake of him to all them that looked for redemption in Jerusalem" (verse 38). We must emphasize the last sentence, which reveals she did not broadcast the news about the Messiah to all people but she "spake of him to all them that looked for redemption in Jerusalem."

It should not surprise us, therefore, that many theologians and pastors today deliberately neglect the prophetic Word. Our message that Jesus is coming soon is falling upon deaf ears; thus, we must redirect the message of Jesus' coming and target only those who are looking for Him.

Paul emphasized, "So that ye come behind in no gift; waiting for the coming of our Lord Jesus Christ" (1 Corinthians 1:7). He confirms that waiting for Jesus to return is a gift from God. These things go hand in hand. Of Simeon, the waiting one, we read, "and the Holy Ghost was upon him." And Anna was completely dedicated to serving the Lord. Our understanding of Bible prophecy must be synchronized with our service for the Lord. The more we serve Him, the more fully we will grasp the spiritual significance behind the fulfillment of Bible prophecy!

CHAPTER 2

UNDERSTANDING PROPHECY

Many people believe that Bible prophecy is too complex to understand so we should just leave it to the "experts." But prophecy can be easily — perhaps we should say readily — understood when paired with some common sense. The Bible doesn't say that God gave prophecies only to theologians and Bible scholars, but "unto his servants things which must shortly come to pass" (Revelation 1:1). In other words, you and I can understand God's prophetic Word, and as we pointed out in Chapter One, God expects us to study it because He is the author of prophecy.

Understanding Prophecy

The parallel existence of the Church of Jesus Christ and the preparation for the Antichrist kingdom on this earth are standard concepts through which Bible prophecy is understood.

Bible prophecy often seems complicated because we fail to consider that some portions of prophecy have already been fulfilled while others will be fulfilled sometime in the future.

For example, John the Baptist's father uttered specific prophecies the day John was born — some of which remain unfulfilled:

> Zacharias was filled with the Holy Ghost, and prophesied, saying, Blessed be the Lord God of Israel; for he hath visited and redeemed his people, and hath raised up an horn of salvation for us in the house of his servant David; As he spake by the mouth of his holy prophets, which have been since the world began: That we should be saved from our enemies, and from the hand of all that hate us; To perform the mercy promised to our fathers, and to remember his holy covenant; The oath which he sware to our father Abraham, That he would grant unto us, that we being delivered out of the hand of our enemies might serve him without fear, In holiness and righteousness before him, all the days of our life. And thou, child, shalt be called the prophet of the Highest: for thou shalt go before the face of the Lord to prepare his ways; To give knowledge of salvation unto his people by the remission of their sins (Luke 1:67-77).

Many portions of this prophecy were not fulfilled during that time, nor have they been fulfilled to this day. Here are some examples:

Israel's Enemies

Verse 71 says that Israel will be "saved from our enemies and from the hand of all that hate us," but this prophecy has not yet been fulfilled. In fact, anti-Semitism is actually increasing. Consider the following media reports:

> **Anti-Semitism on the Rise in America — ADL Survey on Anti-Semitic Attitudes Reveals 17 Percent of Americans Hold "Hardcore" Beliefs**
>
> New York, NY, June 11, 2002...A nationwide survey released today by the Anti-Defamation League (ADL) shows an increase in the number of Americans with anti-Semitic attitudes, reversing a ten-year decline and raising concerns that "an undercurrent of Jewish hatred persists in America. The national poll of 1,000 American adults conducted April 26 through May 6, 2002 found that 17% of Americans — or about 35 million adults — hold views about Jews that are "unquestionably anti-Semitic." Previous surveys commissioned by ADL over the last decade had indicated that anti-Semitism was in decline. A survey of attitudes four years ago found that the number of Americans with hardcore anti-Semitic beliefs had dropped from 20 in 1992, to 12% in 1998. The Anti-Defamation League reports that anti-Semitism in Europe has reached the level of about 30%.

What about Israel's neighbors? The following information comes from the Zionist Organization of America:

Iran's Call for Israel's Destruction — Nothing New In Mid-East

By Morton A. Klein and Dr. Daniel Mandel

Recently, the Iranian president, Mahmoud Ahmadinejad, declared that "Israel must be wiped off the map." Many international leaders reacted appropriately with shock and horror. Yet tragically, such statements in the Arab/Islamic world are nothing new.

From the very day of Israel's establishment to the present day, calls for Israel's violent destruction have been emphatic and continuous across the Middle East. Some examples:

1948: Arab League Secretary-General Azzam Pasha: "This will be a war of extermination and a momentous massacre which will be spoken of like the Mongolian massacres and the Crusades."

1954: Saudi King Saud: "The Arab nations should sacrifice up to 10 million of their 50 million people, if necessary, to wipe out Israel. Israel is to the Arab world a cancer to the human body."

1959: Egyptian President Gamal Abdul Nasser: "I announce from here, on behalf of the United Arab Republic people, that this time we will exterminate Israel."

1967: Iraqi President Abdar-Rahman Aref: "The existence of Israel is a mistake that must be rectified. The clear aim is to wipe Israel off the map."

1980: PLO Chairman Yasser Arafat: "Peace for us means the destruction of Israel. We are preparing for an all-out war, a war which will last for generations."

1993: PLO Chairman Yasser Arafat: "Since we cannot defeat Israel in war we do this in stages. We take any and every territory that we can of Palestine, and establish, sovereignty there and we use it as a springboard to take more. When the time comes, we can get the Arab nations to join us for the final blow against Israel." [Same day of Oslo signing ceremony]

2001: Former Iranian President Hashemi Rafsanjani, "If a day comes when the world of Islam is duly equipped with the arms Israel has in possession, the strategy of colonialism would fact a stalemate because application of an atomic bomb would not leave anything in Israel."

2005: PA Sheikh Ibrahim Mudeiris: "The Jews are a virus resembling AIDS. The day will come when everything will be relieved of the Jews. Listen to the Prophet Muhammad, who tells you about the evil end that awaits Jews. The stones and trees will want the Muslims to finish off every Jew."

2005: Egyptian Muslim Brotherhood leader Muhammad Mehdi Akef, "I declared that we will not recognize Israel which is an alien entity in the region. And we expect the demise of this cancer soon.

"Examples like these are rampant. As the record shows, loathing of Jews and Israel and a desire to destroy them have not evaporated because of formal peace treaties with Egypt and Jordan, the Oslo peace process, the creation of the Palestinian Authority (PA) on land handed over by Israel or

> anything else. The opposite: Arab and Muslim rejection of Israel has seeped across the globe so that even in the gentlemanly halls of American academe, professors like the late Edward Said of Columbia University and Tony Judt of New York University have openly embraced the idea of dismantling Israel.

Another Unfulfilled Prophecy

Israel still doesn't serve God today; the Jews are blind to their Messiah, just as stated in Romans 11:28: "As concerning the gospel, they are enemies for your sakes: but as touching the election, they are beloved for the fathers' sakes."

Zacharias the priest prophesied, "That he would grant unto us, that we being delivered out of the hand of our enemies might serve him without fear, in holiness and righteousness before him, all the days of our life" (Luke 1:74-75).

We know that this part of his prophecy has not yet been fulfilled. The Jews have not been delivered from their enemies, nor are they serving God in holiness and righteousness.

The following verses, however, were fulfilled at that time:

> And thou, child, shalt be called the prophet of the Highest: for thou shalt go before the face of the Lord to prepare his ways; To give knowledge of salvation unto his people by the remission of their sins, through the tender mercy of our God;

> whereby the dayspring from on high hath visited us, to give light to them that sit in darkness and in the shadow of death, to guide our feet into the way of peace (Luke 1:76-79).

Thus, we can see from these verses that prophecy is not limited to an all-at-once fulfillment. This prophecy was made almost 2,000 years ago — part of it was fulfilled, other parts of it will be fulfilled in the future.

Jesus' Messianic Proclamation

Another striking example of a partially fulfilled prophecy is one that Dr. Wim Malgo, founder of Midnight Call Ministries, used as an illustration. In Luke 4 we read that Jesus went to Nazareth and attended the local synagogue where He read the Scripture for that day:

> And he came to Nazareth, where he had been brought up: and, as his custom was, he went into the synagogue on the sabbath day, and stood up for to read. Then the rabbi in charge handed him the book, and He began to read: The Spirit of the Lord is upon me, because he hath anointed me to preach the gospel to the poor; he hath sent me to heal the broken-hearted, to preach deliverance to the captives, and recovering of sight to the blind, to set at liberty them that are bruised, To preach the acceptable year of the Lord. And he closed the book, and he gave it again to the minister, and sat down. And the eyes of all them that were in the synagogue were fas-

> tened on him. And he began to say unto them, This day is this scripture fulfilled in your ears (Luke 4:16, 18-21).

Jesus quoted Isaiah 61:1-2:

> The Spirit of the Lord GOD is upon me; because the LORD hath anointed me to preach good tidings unto the meek; he hath sent me to bind up the brokenhearted, to proclaim liberty to the captives, and the opening of the prison to them that are bound; to proclaim the acceptable year of the LORD, and the day of vengeance of our God; to comfort all that mourn.

Notice the difference here: Isaiah said, "To proclaim the acceptable year of the LORD, and the day of vengeance of our God" but Jesus didn't read the last part of that verse in the synagogue on that Sabbath day. He stopped after reading, "to preach the acceptable year of the Lord." He closed the book, gave it to the rabbi and sat down. Then He said something extremely significant: "This day is this Scripture fulfilled in your ears." The Lord Jesus came to this earth to offer salvation to mankind. He came to fulfill that which was written of Him by the prophets, but He did not come to execute "the day of vengeance of our God" at that time — that is yet to come.

Isaiah's prophecy views Jesus' First and Second Comings as one event. The 2,000 years hidden in between — "the acceptable year of the Lord" and "the day of vengeance of our God" — is the time of the Church. The "day of vengeance" will begin only after the Church has left this earth to meet Jesus in the clouds.

Fear of the Unknown

Simple recognition that the prophecies we have just considered have only been partially fulfilled make their meaning even clearer. Believers have no reason to fear. God has clearly revealed in His Word that those who continue in their unbelief are the ones who should be afraid!

Fear of the unknown can cause many people to deliberately avoid any attempts to understand Bible prophecy. But our attitude toward the prophetic Word, — positive or negative — will not stop its fulfillment. Those people who reject, or who choose to ignore the prophetic Word, cannot be informed of or properly prepared for that which is to come. We would have every reason to fear the events that will come upon the world if we didn't have a clear understanding of the prophetic Word. Here is an example:

> Despite recent improvements in the health of our much brooded — over environment, psychologists, sociologists and epidemiologists say we may well be the most anxious, frightened society in our history. Why are we so scared — and so often scared of the wrong things? Many say the news media is largely to blame. The media, after all, pays the most attention to

> those substances, issues and situations that most frighten their readers and viewers.Thus, almost every day, we read, see and hear about a new purported threat to our health and safety.[1]

While we may admit that the world has a legitimate reason to fear the events that are taking place in the world, Christians have no need to fear. We will only be overtaken by fear if we fail to study the prophetic Word.

The Apostle Peter offers proper advice, which will not lead us into fear of the unknown but will make our hearts rejoice: "We have also a more sure word of prophecy; whereunto ye do well that ye take heed, as unto a light that shineth in a dark place, until the day dawn, and the day star arise in your hearts" (2 Peter 1:19). Fear of the unknown does not justify neglect. On the contrary, if a person ignores the prophetic Word, he will suffer needless fear and miss out on the joy that comes with full immersion in the Word of God!

The Wrong Place at the Wrong Time

We will be in the right place *all* the time when we devote ourselves to the truth of the prophetic Word, which offers absolute assurance of things to come. When we choose not to believe, or to ignore the prophetic Word, we enter foreign territory and will become overwhelmed with fear.

Allow me to recall a harrowing experience I had as a young man in Melbourne, Australia.

On this occasion, nightfall came much too quickly. It seemed as if the day had plunged into sudden darkness. What was even more frightening was the silence that gave my friend, Dieter Fromm, and me an eerie feeling that something was wrong.

Dieter and I were two 19-year-old immigrants from Germany who had no command of the English language other than the few sentences we learned on board the *Castel Felicia*. It took five weeks for the immigrant ship to sail from Germany to Melbourne. One particular English sentence — "This is an apple" — stuck in my mind only because I thought it was so silly.

It didn't take long for us to realize that you cannot walk the streets of a big city with the knowledge of only these four words and expect to find a place to stay for the night much less a job. That was why we left the secure immigration camp some 240 km away and hitchhiked to Melbourne. Of course, we were warned at the Bonnegilla camp not to leave the compound. "The government will take care of you. You will get a job, learn the language, and make money" was what we were told. It was difficult to find comfort in such promises because jobs in Germany were available in abundance. You could literally quit one job, walk across the street and be hired by another firm, so the warning not to strike out on our own seemed meaningless to us. But because we did not heed this warning, we found ourselves in an awkward situation many miles away from the camp.

We thought something strange might have happened in the city because it appeared deserted. We didn't know that it was normal for an Australian city to be virtually empty after business hours. In Europe, people lived in the city in apartments above stores and offices, but downtown Melbourne was strictly for business and when business was over the people left for their homes in the suburbs. Thus, the frightening silence contributed to our feelings of fear. A city without people was incomprehensible to us.

We were lost, hungry, had little money and nowhere to sleep. Suddenly, in the darkness of this strange city, we noticed what appeared to be a vacant building. Luckily, the door was left open, and with the exception of a few frightened rats, we felt rather safe after closing the door.

We spotted a stack of old newspapers among the trash, and after we ate our last candy bar, we used the newspapers as blankets. "The world will look different tomorrow," we thought. Surely we would find a job at one of the nearby construction sites.

The cold woke us up sometime that night, so we took our paper blankets and climbed the broken stairs in search of warmer temperatures. Not long after that, however, we were awakened by the sound of a car, a sound we had not heard the previous evening. Strangely, the motor stopped, and a car door opened and closed right in front of our building!

We jumped up and ran to the window. Our hearts began to beat faster when the door downstairs was opened and someone walked in. The two of us searched the room for any object suitable to defend ourselves against the intruder. We believed our lives were really in danger.

My thoughts immediately focused on the many times in my young life that I had narrowly escaped death. For example, our entire family nearly starved to death because of a curfew the Russians had imposed in 1944. We lost my youngest sister through that ordeal.

In a separate event, Germans were being executed at random by the victorious communist forces, but they stopped killing just short of where we were staying. At this point, I was prepared for virtually anything to happen, but the minutes felt like an eternity.

We heard each footstep and waited in suspense for the sounds to move up the stairs. Silence — then we heard the sound of crumpling newspaper. It sounded like the paper was thrown in the direction of the stairs. The suspense was so great that we could hear our own hearts beating.

We heard the sound of a striking match above our own heartbeats. Suddenly it became clear that this fellow was not after us — he didn't even know anyone else was in the building! Maybe the owner of the building wanted it burned down so that he could collect the insurance money.

But what about us? Should we try to stop him? We wouldn't stand a chance against him if he had a gun. We could easily be silenced — two witnesses conveniently disappearing in the fire.

We started to smell smoke. Our desperation grew. If we did nothing, we would die but if we did something, we still might die. Then the long silence was broken by the sound of footsteps. The door closed downstairs. What a relief! Now we were free to act. Dieter quickly jumped to the window to steal a glance at the man who hastily jumped into his British MG through the open roof. The engine revved up and the car sped out of sight.

By the time we had reached the ground floor, the fire had already started to consume the wooden staircase. Our next decision took only seconds — we extinguished the fire.

Exhausted, we walked the sidewalks of this strange city, happy to be alive. The arsonist must have waited in anticipation for the smoke to appear in his rearview mirror, or hear the fire alarm ring, but it wasn't going to happen, at least not on that night!

We had considered letting the fire burn, but our presence in the city may have left us open to suspicion. Any law enforcement officer could immediately identify us as the arsonists because we were in the building. We were in the wrong place at the wrong time, we spoke no English and we had no money. It would have been assumed that we started the fire to keep warm, and that it had gotten out of hand. We were pleased with our decision to put out the fire; now we were filled with hope for the new day that was ahead of us.

Lost in Foreign Territory

Why am I writing about this experience in a chapter that focuses on understanding prophecy? I have done so intentionally to demonstrate that we were in the wrong place at the wrong time, and ended up in an extremely dangerous situation because we were navigating territory we had no business being in.

And in the same manner, this example should serve as a reminder to us that anyone who is without Christ is totally lost and on his way to eternal damnation. The Bible states that separation from God is forever for those who die without Christ.

If Dieter and I had known the language, we could have asked someone where we could find a place to stay. We could have easily avoided the terrible situation in which we had found ourselves.

This experience applies equally to everyone who fails to heed the prophetic Word: they walk in darkness and are oppressed by an unnecessary fear.

Eternal Security in Christ

Read the guarantee John wrote in the precious Word of God:

> Let not your heart be troubled: ye believe in God, believe also in me. In my Father's house are many mansions: if it were not so, I would have told you. I go to prepare a place for you. And if I go and prepare a place for you, I will come again, and receive you unto myself; that where I am, there ye may be also. And whither I go ye know, and the way ye know (John 14:1-4).

This is not some kind of cheap advertising, promotional material, or Madison Avenue propaganda. This is a promise from the living Christ who made heaven and earth and all that is within.

Are you a child of God? Then have no fear. Read the book of Revelation, which God has given as a forecast of the future. In fact, God makes a wonderful promise to those who read this book: "Blessed is he that readeth, and they that hear the words of this prophecy, and keep those things which are written therein: for the time is at hand" (Revelation 1:3).

The study of the prophetic Word, therefore, should not be taken lightly, and its interpretation does not have to be left to the "specialists" — it is addressed to every child of God.

The prophetic Word is an assurance of things to come and it provides us with the hope and comfort that Jesus could indeed come today!

CHAPTER 3

ERRORS OF INTERPRETATION

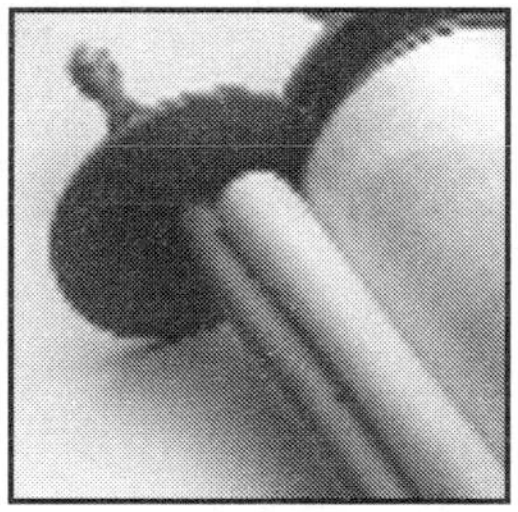

As you read this chapter, you will understand some of the false interpretations of prophecies that were popularized following Israel's famous "Six Day War" in 1967. The analysis provided in this chapter should settle the rumors about the "beast computer" in Belgium, the miraculous multiplication of vultures, the continuous claims of discovery of the Ark of the Covenant and Noah's Ark. Such claims are not helpful, but only contribute to the growing confusion in today's world.

Errors of Interpretation

God's Word says that to understand Jesus is to understand prophecy. For example, Revelation 19:10 states: "And I fell at his feet to worship him. And he said unto me, See thou do it not: I am thy fellowservant, and of thy brethren that have the testimony of Jesus: worship God: for the testimony of Jesus is the spirit of prophecy." Let me repeat the last sentence: "For the testimony of Jesus is the spirit of prophecy." This is an overwhelming announcement that comes directly from heaven and bears witness once again to the trinity of the Godhead.

In unmistakable terms, the perfect unity of the Father, Son and Holy Spirit in conjunction with prophecy is demonstrated here.

Jesus is truth, the Spirit is truth and prophecy is truth. Therefore, when we are dealing with the prophetic Word, we must keep in mind that we are dealing with the God of prophecy, with Jesus, and with the Spirit of truth!

The testimony of Jesus Christ is truth, regardless of whether or not we believe it to be true. Our unbelief or misinterpretation does not change the truth.

One Way to Salvation

No one can be saved but through Jesus Christ. God's Word says that He is the way, the truth, and the life, and that no one comes to the Father but by Him. This testimony of Jesus Christ is true for all mankind—past, present, and future. The blood of the Lamb is the only substance that cleanses a sinner completely and perfectly, allowing him to stand guiltless before the Creator.

We may freely interpret endtime signs in Scripture, but our interpretation must never be considered the final authority. We must allow Scripture to interpret Scripture just as the Lord Jesus and His apostles did. Confusion will always arise when we fail to follow this rule of thumb.

For example, consider the following news article from the January 3, 1994 edition of *The Scotsman:*

> A fresh dispute over Bible stories has split the Church of Scotland after the moderator described the virgin birth as a symbolic event and attacked religious conservatives. Preaching in Edinburgh, the Rt. Rev. Dr. James Weatherhead, Moderator of the General Assembly, defended controversial doubts recently voiced by church figures, including the Bishop of Durham, over the factual reality of the virgin birth. Dr. Weatherhead, speaking at St. Giles' Cathedral, said the Bible was much more a poetic document than one with legal or literal truths. "We are not necessarily saying anything derogatory at all about the virgin birth if we say it is a symbol," he said [2]

In this case a prominent theologian becomes a fool by denying the literal truth of the Bible in his claim that the virgin birth is merely symbolic.

The Church is the Recipient of Prophecy

The Apostle Peter admonishes believers to take heed of the prophetic Word and he emphasizes its reliability. The Holy Spirit inspired him to write this profound verse: "Knowing this first, that no prophecy of the scripture is of any private interpretation" (2 Peter 1:20). The prophetic Word has been given to the Church of Jesus Christ — the entire body of believers; therefore, Scripture is not open to private interpretation. When an individual believes he has recognized a special truth in Scripture, he should carefully compare his belief with other men of God and consider how they have interpreted the same passage of Scripture. For example, the Spirit of prophecy emphasizes to so many servants of God that the time of the Gentiles is coming to an end. The Church has received this knowledge; it was not a special revelation that was given to one certain person to recognize it as fact.

The Apostle Peter emphasized that the Word of prophecy was inspired by God the Holy Spirit — it did not come about by men, "For the prophecy came not in old time by the will of man: but holy men of God spake as they were moved by the Holy Ghost" (2 Peter 1:21).

Prophecies about Jerusalem

Let's look at some prophecies that are being emphasized by the body of believers in Christ today.

Jerusalem has become an increasingly burdensome stone for the nations. Such understanding does not need special interpretation; this prophecy is open for all believers. The following example should be recognized as being part of the process leading up to the fulfillment of the prophecy regarding the Holy City.

> Jerusalem should be the peaceful meeting place for... all the children of Abraham, Arabs and Jews alike. But there can be no sovereignty over Jerusalem's holy sites except by the Almighty. I've suggested that a learned group representing all schools within the Islamic world enter an interfaith dialogue with the Christian and Jewish worlds to seek a formula preserving rights and protecting the holy places for all three great monotheistic religions. But I've never suggested that Jerusalem be divided.[3]

It appears that the king of Jordan is acting as a spokesman for ecumenism between Jews, Arabs and Christians!

On the other hand, we hear other voices—Arab Palestinians—quoted in an article on page 4 of the June 17, 1995 issue of *The Jerusalem Post International Edition:*

> About 10,000 members of the Islamic Movement attended a "Jerusalem First" rally in Kafar Kassem to demand that eastern Jerusalem be made the capital of a Palestinian state. 'The Israeli government and the Likud have agreed on a

> fact, agreeing that there are two peoples here who share one homeland, and each people must be given its own independent state,' said Abdullah Nimr Darwish, the head of the Islamic Movement. 'This is why we say that Jerusalem's status cannot be harmed. Jerusalem first must be, as far as the Palestinian nation is concerned, the capital of the Palestinian state that will emerge,' he said [4]

As far as the nations are concerned, virtually all of them have their embassies in Tel Aviv rather than in Jerusalem, the capital of the Jewish state, because they believe Jerusalem should be an international city and not the capital of a Jewish state. The Bible clearly predicts that Jerusalem will become the center of controversy in the endtimes, thus we know we are approaching the final stages of the last days.

Prophecies about the State of Israel

God started something new when the State of Israel was established; therefore, the day of the Church's completion from among the Gentiles cannot be too far in the future.

I write this because the Church and Israel cannot co-exist for an extended period of time. Israel was being dispersed when the Church began and now Israel is being re-gathered so the Church must be removed.

Countless servants of God agree that we are in the last stages of the endtimes and the nation and land of

Israel are visible markers of Bible prophecy fulfillment. We cannot ignore the fact that Israel is the fulfillment of Bible prophecy even in its current state of unbelief.

I won't go into detail here, but Ezekiel 36 explains that when the Jews return to Israel in unbelief, the land that once was a desert will be productive again, and the dispersed shall return and multiply. These are undeniable facts, which we will deal with later in this book.

Sensationalism: A Stumbling Stone in Prophecy

Let us now consider the dangers of misinterpretation and rumor.

Israel captured the entire Sinai Peninsula from Egypt and took all of the Golan Heights, Judea and Samaria from Syria. Israel's greatest reward, however, was the liberation of eastern Jerusalem. Thus, the city was united once again.

Temple Stones

After the Jews celebrated their victory at the Wailing Wall— the final remnant of the western retaining wall of the temple mount— rumors started to circulate that Israel was planning to rebuild the temple.

Articles were published in Christian publications alleging that stones for the temple were cut and ready to be shipped to Israel at any given time. It was reported that the temple stones were cut in a rock quarry in Bedford, Indiana. After some research, the story was found to be a rumor.

Comments from Israel included this one: "Stones are the last thing we need. If we could export ours, we would be the richest country on the face of the earth."

Nevertheless, the temple will be built. Even today, a number of Jewish groups such as the Temple Mount Faithful are trying to do everything in their power to have the temple built on Mount Moriah. The Temple Mount Institute is preparing temple utensils and training young men as priests in accordance with the levitical law, so that trained priests will handle the services when the temple is built. Although preparations for the temple are being made, we must add that Israel's powerful religious authority does not officially recognize doing so. Nevertheless, it does reveal that there are certain Jews who take the rebuilding of the temple on Mount Moriah seriously. Naturally, it is all but impossible at this point in time to even attempt to rebuild the temple because the temple mount is subject to Islamic law. Nevertheless, the present conflict between Israel and the Arabs could change quickly. We must never underestimate the potential of political surprises.

Miraculous Multiplication of Vultures

Another sensational rumor revolves around the anticipated invasion of Israel by a northern confederacy as described in Ezekiel 38 and 39. Ezekiel 39:17 reads: "And, thou son of man, thus saith the Lord GOD; Speak unto every feathered fowl, and to every beast of the field, Assemble yourselves, and come; gather yourselves on every side to my sacrifice that I do sacrifice for you, even a great sacrifice upon the mountains of Israel, that ye may eat flesh, and drink blood."

An extensive article included claims that vultures in Israel were multiplying in unusual numbers. The writer of the article speculated that it was in preparation for the great sacrifice recorded in Ezekiel 39:17. The society for the protection of nature in Israel, however, found no evidence to support the alleged increase in the number of vultures.

We must mention that the bird population in Israel has increased, but that is primarily due to the re-vegetation of the land and the countless fishponds that have been built for fish farms. It was reported in *The Jerusalem Post* that Israel has lost more planes due to accidents with birds than they lost during the wars against the Arabs!

The Beast Computer in Belgium

In another article, it was reported that a giant two-story computer, capable of storing information on every person on the earth, was housed in Brussels, the headquarters of the European Commission. The computer was affectionately called "The Beast." This rumor was reported back in the 70's when Europe was five to ten years behind America in computer technology. This story was also exposed as a hoax.

Noah's Ark and Archeological Artifacts

Many books and movies have been written and produced about the discovery of Noah's Ark, the Ark of the Covenant, the gravestones of Mary, Joseph, and many of the apostles, as well as many other supposed great archaeological discoveries. It seems that one sensational discovery is outdone by the next but each one of them has been proven false under further examination. Naturally, that does not mean there haven't been any interesting archaeological discoveries in Israel.

Whether it is the search for the ashes of the red heifer, the discovery of oil in the tribal territory of Asher, or a supposed geological rift that already exists in the Mount of Olives, these exciting stories rekindle people's interest in Bible prophecy. Unfortunately, these stories are generally not based on facts, but are the products of someone's imagination.

Our Lord's return is not contingent upon man's discoveries. Physical discoveries, regardless of their nature, are completely insignificant when compared to Holy Scripture, which is eternal truth and does not need any new discovery in order to be found valid. We possess the full council of God in the 66 books of the Bible! Scripture backed by Scripture provides all the validation necessary.

What We Really Need to Watch

We must pay attention to the reports about Israel's resurrection, the Jewish people's fight for peace, and their desire to join the European Union.

Israel has become a nation just as prophesied. The Jews are returning to Israel from virtually all nations of the world, which is also recorded in Scripture. The Jews will be successful and peace will ultimately be negotiated, although enemies have threatened them — another prophecy. However, they will ultimately accept the false messiah that Jesus prophesied about with the words, "If another shall come in his own name, him ye will receive" (John 5:43). Rumors will only deter us from our serious exposition of the prophetic Word and they must be rejected.

CHAPTER 4

FAMILY CONFLICT IN THE MIDDLE EAST

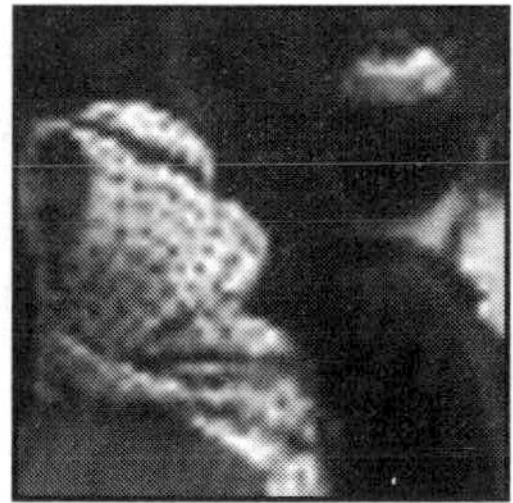

Abraham is called the father of all believers. God used Isaac, Jacob and his descendants to fulfill His intention of establishing the kingdom of God on earth and to offer salvation to mankind. In a compact manner, this chapter explains how Abraham's mistakes contributed to the great conflict that is occurring today in Israel and the Middle East: the Arabs also claim Abraham as their father.

Family Conflict in the Middle East

The 1900s will be known as the most turbulent century in the history of mankind. The first 45 years saw two world wars in which millions of people perished. It was in this century that communism began to flourish in Russia and then spread around the world. But in this century, we also saw the internal collapse of communism, vividly highlighted by the dismantling of the Berlin Wall.

Furthermore, in this century we saw the rise of a sinister spirit that deceived people into believing there was a "Jewish" problem. The same spirit was responsible for the rise of the most hideous anti-Semitic power structure the world has ever known. More than six million Jews perished at the hands of Germany's murderous Nazi regime led by the infamous Adolf Hitler.

The Return of the Jews

In this century we have also witnessed a unique occurrence: the return of the Jews to the land of their fathers. The first Jewish people came to the land at the turn of the 19th century. They joined with those who were already there and began to cultivate the land. Their goal was to revive the land and to produce food for the people who were yet to arrive.

The task looked hopeless in the early days, but the Jews persisted and the fruit of their labor resulted in the eventual founding of the State of Israel on May

14, 1948. Since that time, the focus of attention has shifted dramatically from the new world to the old world, the Middle East, as the center of the future.

Parallel to the development of modern Zionism — with its goal to return Jews to the land of Zion — was the phenomenal explosion in the significance of the Arab nations.

The industrial world unexpectedly found itself at the mercy of Arab leaders who controlled vast resources of oil. While hundreds of books have been written about the Middle East conflict, and an almost inexhaustible volume of documentation is available, I would like to point out in this chapter that the entire conflict is not merely a political, religious, military, or economic one, but is actually a family conflict. Just as two children in a family will fight over one toy, the Jews and Arabs continue to fight over the inheritance: the land of Israel.

Abraham: The Beginning of Israel and the Arabs

The Arab/Jewish conflict began with Abraham, a unique man because he received a very special promise from God the Creator.

Genesis 11 describes man's unsuccessful attempt at world unity in the building of the Tower of Babel, which was supposed to reach up to heaven. Then, in Genesis 12, we read:

> Now the LORD had said unto Abram, Get thee out of thy country, and from thy kindred, and from thy father's house, unto a land that I will shew thee: And I will make of thee a great nation, and I will bless thee, and make thy name great; and thou shalt be a blessing: And I will bless them that bless thee, and curse him that curseth thee: and in thee shall all families of the earth be blessed (Genesis 12:1-3).

This was not some kind of pronouncement of blessing by a priest, a prophet, or some great dignitary, but it came by God's four-fold "I will" to Abraham.

God instructed Abraham to leave everything behind and take a Holy Land journey. He had to leave his country, his family, even his father's house, and travel to a place yet unknown to him. But Abraham trusted the living God who had spoken to Him so he did as he was told.

One of Abraham's unique characteristics was his obedience. He believed God and acted upon that belief. For that reason, we read, "that he [Abraham] might be the father of all them that believe" (Romans 4:11).

Abraham was a faithful servant of the Lord who believed in God more than in anything else. Nevertheless, in some instances, he allowed his flesh to run parallel to his faith life.

Thus the conflict that we see in the Middle East today can be traced back to this great patriarch of the Jews and the Arabs.

Abraham and the Arabs

Sarah ran out of patience first: "And Sarai said unto Abram, Behold now, the LORD hath restrained me from bearing: I pray thee, go in unto my maid; it may be that I may obtain children by her. And Abram hearkened to the voice of Sarai" (Genesis 16:2).

Abraham was 86 years old. Apparently, he had reached the point where he must have thought, "We've got to do something!"

Perhaps he had agreed with Sarah, and thought this to be the way of the Lord, thus, he followed his wife's advice: "And he went in unto Hagar, and she conceived: and when she saw that she had conceived, her mistress was despised in her eyes" (verse 4).

Obviously, this was not what God had intended for them. Hagar hated Sarah. Scripture does not reveal whether or not Abraham and Sarah realized that what they had done was wrong; however, the Lord spoke to Abraham 13 years later and repeated the promise He had made to him years before.

In the meantime, God had changed Abram's name to Abraham. Abram means "father of height" or "high father," and Abraham means "father of a multitude."

Abraham's Prayer for the Arabs

After he received additional instructions, Abraham apparently started to think that God was confirming Ishmael as His chosen seed. He prayed, "O that

Ishmael might live before thee!" (Genesis 17:18).

But God quickly corrected him: "Sarah thy wife shall bear thee a son indeed; and thou shalt call his name Isaac: and I will establish my covenant with him for an everlasting covenant, and with his seed after him" (verse 19).

God specifically stated that He had heard Abraham's prayer for Ishmael, "And as for Ishmael, I have heard thee: Behold, I have blessed him, and will make him fruitful, and will multiply him exceedingly; twelve princes shall he beget, and I will make him a great nation" (verse 20). But, He emphasized that Isaac, not Ishmael, was the covenant bearer: "But my covenant will I establish with Isaac, which Sarah shall bear unto thee at this set time in the next year" (verse 21).

Blessings of Ishmael

Isaac's selection did not detract from the tremendous blessing Ishmael would receive. Ishmael would be fruitful and multiply exceedingly. Ishmael would be the father of twelve princes and would become a great nation.

Genesis 25 contains the fulfillment of this promise. Ishmael's genealogy reveals that twelve princes indeed came forth from him. Ishmael should not be belittled or rejected. God promised the tremendous blessings we have just noted to him and his descendants. Nevertheless, Ishmael's descendants became bitter enemies of Israel (see Judges 8:24 and Psalm 83), and they remain so to this day. A news article reflects this bitterness:

> News photos of Palestinian policemen raising a Nazi-style salute increase anxiety among Holocaust survivors, according to a Bikur Holim Hospital psychiatrist who researched survivors' ability to cope with the present. Dr. Yehudit Rappaports and Dr. Shalom Robinson of the Center for Holocaust Studies found their subjects through Yad Vashem. Those interviewed said anything that reminded them of the Nazi era — including the picture of Nazi-style salutes by Palestinian policemen in Gaza published in the papers — intensified their suffering.[5]

Abraham's Other Descendants

Abraham must have felt like his calling was completed after sending his servant to find a wife for his son Isaac. After Isaac married Rebekah, Genesis 25: 1-6 reports:

> Then again Abraham took a wife, and her name was Keturah. And she bare him Zimran, and Jokshan, and Medan, and Midian, and Ishbak, and Shuah. And Jokshan begat Sheba, and Dedan. And the sons of Dedan were Asshurim, and Letushim, and Leummim. And the sons of Midian; Ephah, and Epher, and Hanoch, and Abidah, and Eldaah. All these were the children of Keturah. And Abraham gave all that he had unto Isaac. But unto the sons of the concubines, which Abraham had, Abraham gave gifts, and sent them away from Isaac his son, while he yet lived, eastward, unto the east country.

Abraham raised another family in his old age!

We learn from the genealogy of this family that Abraham's sons with Keturah also became bitter enemies of Israel. Therefore, we see again that the Arabs do indeed belong to the same family and they are related to Israel.

Abraham and 666

It is interesting that Abraham's death is recorded in the 666th verse of the Old Testament. Genesis 25:7-8 reads: "And these are the days of the years of Abraham's life which he lived, an hundred threescore and fifteen years. Then Abraham gave up the ghost, and died in a good old age, an old man, and full of years; and was gathered to his people."

When I noticed that the end of Abraham's life is recorded in verse 666 of the Old Testament (naturally I am aware that verses were not numbered in the original manuscripts) I became curious of what event would be recorded in verse 666 of the New Testament — it was as Matthew 20:18, where Jesus describes His impending death: "Behold, we go up to Jerusalem; and the Son of man shall be betrayed unto the chief priests and unto the scribes, and they shall condemn him to death" (Matthew 20:18).

The difference, however, lays in the fact that Jesus prophesied His own death while Abraham did not.

Redemption in Prophecy

God would use Abraham and his seed to reveal how He would redeem mankind from Satan's oppression and from the bondage of sin.

The possibility of Abraham becoming the patriarch of a great nation became a reality after the promised offspring was born. But then we read a shocking statement addressed to him: "Take now thy son, thine only son Isaac, whom thou lovest, and get thee into the land of Moriah; and offer him there for a burnt offering upon one of the mountains which I will tell thee of" (Genesis 22:2). We must emphasize the words, "thine only son Isaac, whom thou lovest." God did not mention Ishmael, but specifically identified Isaac as Abraham's only son and heir to the promise. It reminds us of the Lord Jesus Christ, of whom God said, "This is my beloved Son, in whom I am well pleased" (Matthew 17:5).

Abraham's Difficult Time

Abraham was instructed to commit an unthinkable act: he was commanded to offer his most precious possession, his only beloved son, as God told him to sacrifice Isaac as a burnt offering.

Wouldn't it have been natural at such a crucial time to have at least called upon the elders of his household to discuss the matter? Would it not have been appropriate to inform Sarah of God's shocking command? Perhaps they should have started a prayer meeting to seek confirmation that this really was God's will. Maybe Abraham misunderstood. After all, he was an old man, and perhaps he heard incorrectly. Maybe he had a bad dream.

Many options were available to avoid the impossible situation. "Under no circumstances should Isaac die," they must have thought. After all, he was the answer to their prayers, he was the promised son and only he could fulfill God's pledge that Abraham's seed would become a great nation.

Abraham's Obedience

How did Abraham react? "And Abraham rose up early in the morning" (Genesis 22:3). Abraham believed God in spite of the potentially terrifying consequences. This was no mistake. Abraham was in tune with God — he had perfect fellowship with Him. God knew what He was saying and Abraham had absolute certainty of his relationship, which gave him assurance to act in perfect accordance with the word God spoke! Thus, in Abraham we see a prophetic picture of God's love: "For God so loved the world, that he gave his only begotten Son, that whosoever believeth in him should not perish, but have everlasting life" (John 3:16). Abraham was also willing to give up his own son!

We know how the story ended. Abraham did not have to sacrifice Isaac, but God provided a substitute: "And Abraham lifted up his eyes, and looked, and behold behind him a ram caught in a thicket by his horns: and Abraham went and took the ram, and offered him up for a burnt offering in the stead of his son" (Genesis 22:13).

Abraham's Errors

Although Abraham believed in God and acted in accordance with his belief, he also made mistakes, as we have seen in the case of Ishmael. Abraham was a human being; he lived in the real world and had to make decisions, care for his family, plan for the future, and manage his little empire.

Parallel to his faithfulness and obedience, he also had to think for himself. Traveling back in time to Genesis 12:4, we read: "So Abram departed, as the LORD had spoken unto him; and Lot went with him: and Abram was seventy and five years old when he departed out of Haran." This 75-year-old man received a tremendous promise from God, but then we read, "Lot went with him."

The text does not reveal whether Abraham urged him to come or whether Lot went voluntarily. It is reasonable to assume that this was one way to assure that the younger Lot would bring forth descendants that could fulfill the promise that Abraham's family would produce a great nation.

But didn't God clearly instruct Abraham to separate himself from his relatives, parents and siblings? Abraham did everything right, except when it came to tag-along Lot.

Lot Chose the Left

This little family union did not last long. The Bible reports, "And there was a strife between the herdmen of Abram's cattle and the herdmen of Lot's cattle: and the Canaanite and the Perizzite dwelled then in the land" (Genesis 13:7). Again, we see Abraham deal wisely and generously with Lot. Let's read the story:

> And Abram said unto Lot, Let there be no strife, I pray thee, between me and thee, and between my herdmen and thy herdmen; for we be brethren. Is not the whole land before thee? separate thyself, I pray thee, from me: if thou wilt take the left hand, then I will go to the right; or if thou depart to the right hand, then I will go to the left. And Lot lifted up his eyes, and beheld all the plain of Jordan, that it was well watered every where, before the LORD destroyed Sodom and Gomorrah, even as the garden of the LORD, like the land of Egypt, as thou comest unto Zoar. Then Lot chose him all the plain of Jordan; and Lot journeyed east: and they separated themselves the one from the other (Genesis 13:8-11).

Lot didn't prosper because he acted on what he saw rather than by faith: "And Lot lifted up his eyes." He chose what was most pleasing to his eyes. There was no evidence of faith on Lot's part. Out of respect for his uncle, Lot should have at least offered

Abraham first dibs on the land spread out before them. Lot's greed, however, resulted in his later having to be saved from the wickedness of Sodom and Gomorrah by God's intercession on behalf of Abraham's prayer.

Lot left behind a shameful legacy, as reported in Genesis 19:36-38:

> Thus were both the daughters of Lot with child by their father. And the firstborn bare a son, and called his name Moab: the same is the father of the Moabites unto this day. And the younger, she also bare a son, and called his name Benammi: the same is the father of the children of Ammon unto this day.

The Moabites and the Ammonites later became bitter enemies of Israel. Thus we see the beginning of another family conflict in the Middle East. This family feud continues to this day; sometimes fought with weapons of war and other times with words.

The following two news articles reflect the severity of the conflict that has gone on for so long, but through negotiation is now coming to an end.

> Dear Citizens of Israel,
>
> We are adding today another rung in the rising ladder towards the realization of the dream of peace. Full peace with Jordan is attainable. We shall work with Jordan to bring it to fruition.
>
> We all embrace today the Washington Declaration. Israelis, Jordanians, all the lovers of peace and freedom in the world.

> Tomorrow morning we shall all awaken to a new page in our history. And on this we can say: "This is the day which the LORD hath made; we will rejoice and be glad in it" (Psalm 118:24).
>
> Good evening to you there at home, in Israel. Tomorrow, I hope everything can be different. Peaceful greetings to you from the peace-making. [Prime Minister Rabin speaking from Washington on the eve of the Israeli/Jordanian agreement, July 24, 1994.] [6]

> Instead of visions of blood and tears there will rise visions of happiness and beauty, life and peace. We are at a historic crossroad. Do we choose the path of the tongues of fire, billowing smoke and rivers of blood, or of blooming deserts, restored wastelands, progress, growth, justice and freedom?
>
> The world has tipped in the direction of economics rather than military might. Armies conquer physical entities, but they cannot conquer qualitative ones. At this stage of the game, objects that may be subject to a military takeover are no longer of value. [Israeli Foreign Minister Shimon Peres] [7]

This peace process will end in peace for Jews, Arabs and Christians in the Middle East and will ultimately affect the entire world. But we must emphasize that this peace will only be temporary because the cause for this division among these people has not been removed. Sin is the cause and it has never been dealt with in any political process.

Only when Jesus returns and puts an end to the

powers of darkness, destroying the wicked with His appearance, will He establish everlasting peace. Jesus alone paid the price for lasting peace — He removed the cause of conflict: sin.

Lot's Descendants Oppose Israel

Also important to note is that approximately 1,500 years after Abraham, the prophet Ezekiel wrote that the Moabites and Ammonites openly expressed their pleasure in Israel's misfortune, which greatly displeased the Lord.

The statements made by the Ammonites and the Moabites regarding Judah and Israel were true — Israel had indeed sinned greatly. The house of the Lord was profaned, the land had become desolate, and Israel and Judah were led into captivity. But the Ammonites and Moabites made the mistake of comparing God's chosen people to others. Ezekiel 25:8 reads: "Thus saith the Lord GOD; Because that Moab and Seir do say, Behold, the house of Judah is like unto all the heathen."

To gain a better insight, let's read additional verses to fully understand God's displeasure with the Ammonites and Moabites:

> The word of the LORD came again unto me, saying, Son of man, set thy face against the Ammonites, and prophesy against them; And say unto the Ammonites, Hear the word of the Lord GOD; Thus saith the Lord GOD; Because thou saidst,

> Aha, against my sanctuary, when it was profaned; and against the land of Israel, when it was desolate; and against the house of Judah, when they went into captivity. For thus saith the Lord GOD; Because thou hast clapped thine hands, and stamped with the feet, and rejoiced in heart with all thy despite against the land of Israel (Ezekiel 25:1-3,6).

Here is God's answer, which clearly reveals that no one, not even relatives, have the right to judge Israel:

> Therefore, behold, I will open the side of Moab from the cities, from his cities which are on his frontiers, the glory of the country, Bethjeshimoth, Baalmeon, and Kiriathaim, Unto the men of the east with the Ammonites, and will give them in possession, that the Ammonites may not be remembered among the nations. And I will execute judgments upon Moab; and they shall know that I am the LORD (verses 9-11).

The Apple of His Eye

We often hear statements, even from Christians, that the Jews crucified Jesus, they rejected the Messiah, and they were cast out into the nations of the world and became a reproach because of their sins. Some will even go so far as to say Hitler was right in persecuting the Jews so that they would go back to the land of Israel and fulfill Bible prophecy when they reestablished the nation on Israeli soil!

To make such statements, or to even think in such a way, is extremely dangerous, as we have just read in Ezekiel 25. Actually, the Lord is very sensitive regarding His people: "For thus saith the LORD of hosts; after the glory hath he sent me unto the nations which spoiled you: for he that toucheth you toucheth the apple of his eye" (Zechariah 2:8). Everyone knows how sensitive an organ the eye is — a tiny speck of dust can irritate it, yet here we see that God says, "For he that toucheth you toucheth the apple of his eye."

Of course, Israel had sinned greatly. The Jews cried, "Crucify him!" They shouted, "We have no king but Caesar!" And God threatened severe punishment upon the Jewish people. Woe unto those people who became tools of the punishment. Jesus said, "It is impossible but that offences will come: but woe unto him, through whom they come!" (Luke 17:1).

God's Sore Displeasure

You can sense God's outrage at the behavior of the heathen when He emphasizes His love for Zion: "So the angel that communed with me said unto me, Cry thou, saying, Thus saith the LORD of hosts; I am jealous for Jerusalem and for Zion with a great jealousy" (Zechariah 1:14). In the next verse He explains the reason for His jealousy and displeasure with the heathen: "And I am very sore displeased with the heathen that are at ease: for I was but a little displeased, and they helped forward the affliction" (Zechariah 1:15).

Let me give you an example. Assume we are next-door neighbors. You have an unruly child whose behavior has become so offensive to me that I walk over to your house, grab your child and spank him! You would certainly find my behavior offensive, and rightly so, because your children are your responsibility and not mine. He may have deserved punishment because of his bad behavior, but it certainly was not my place to take matters into my own hand and spank him.

Now apply this same line of reasoning to Israel. The Jews have indeed sinned against God. In fact, each of their violations against God's holy covenant is listed throughout the Bible. God used each of the prophets to pronounce judgment upon the Jews. Yet He says, "I was but a little displeased [with Israel] and they [the nations] helped forward the affliction" (Zechariah 1:15). Israel's sin did not negate God's love for His people Israel.

We could fill countless pages with a list of the sins Israel has committed against the living God, who led them out of slavery in Egypt. That, however, does not change God's eternal resolutions.

He spared judgment upon Israel through the blood of a lamb, which the Israelites applied to the door-posts and lintels of their homes; thus, the angel of death passed over them. How mightily He led them through the Red Sea as if they walked on dry ground! The Egyptian army that pursued them had perished in the waters and yet they still refused to heed the Word of God.

Nevertheless, this conflict remains a family affair that involves God and His own people. While God reveals the details of Israel's sin and threatens them with the wrath of His judgment, we see a totally different picture when viewed from the outside.

Two Views of Israel

Let's look at Israel from God's perspective. Notice that this conflict is an internal matter:

> And the LORD said unto Moses, How long will this people provoke me? and how long will it be ere they believe me, for all the signs which I have shewed among them? . . . Because all those men which have seen my glory, and my miracles, which I did in Egypt and in the wilderness, and have tempted me now these ten times, and have not hearkened to my voice (Numbers 14:11, 22).

Now let us observe Israel from the outside — from a Gentile point of view. In Numbers 23 it appears that the prophet Balaam is talking about some other nation, not the rebellious nation of Israel. Read his words:

> He hath not beheld iniquity in Jacob, neither hath he seen perverseness in Israel: the LORD his God is with him, and the shout of a king is among them. God brought them out of Egypt; he hath as it were the strength of an unicorn. Surely

> there is no enchantment against Jacob, neither is there any divination against Israel: according to this time it shall be said of Jacob and of Israel, What hath God wrought! Behold, the people shall rise up as a great lion, and lift up himself as a young lion: he shall not lie down until he eat of the prey, and drink the blood of the slain (Numbers 23:21-24).

This passage certainly does not fit the description of a rebellious Israel but it *is* Israel. Only when we understand the high calling of the Jewish people will we be able to grasp the progression of the prophetic Word in relation to endtime events.

Two Views of Your Family

To other people, your family may appear to be living in harmony with each other. You maintain your property, go to work, pay your bills and taxes, send your children to school, dress them properly, and attend church regularly, but no one knows what is really happening within the four walls of your home. There may be strife, jealousy, bitterness, and fighting to the extent that your family is on the brink of falling apart. But it is *your* house, and it is *your* family. You alone are responsible for your family. You may ask someone for advice but no one has the right to come into your home and tell you what to do.

In most cases, tribulation within a family does not last indefinitely, especially when one or both spouses is walking with the Lord. You make a decision and say, "Lord, I love you with all my heart. I want to do your will in spite of the fact that I am failing on a daily basis and I no longer have power within my own house. My heart aches over the many miseries I have created within our family. Lord, I totally trust that you will restore my family." The Lord knows, He forgives, and He heals, because you thrust yourself into His loving arms!

Walking Wisely Amid Difficult Circumstances

Dear friend, please remember that when you walk wisely in the midst of your difficulties, and remember that you are a child of God, then the world can only see that which Balaam saw of the people of Israel. You will then walk in the victory of the Lord Jesus Christ. You will be a light to the world and salt to the earth, regardless of the circumstances in which you find yourself.

These examples should clearly show that Israel is God's business. He has chosen the Jewish people. They are His family, His responsibility, and He will bring to pass all the promises that He has ever made to them!

The Arabs Today

The Arab nations had been disregarded for many centuries, and suffered greatly under occupation from Britain, France, and other European nations. These people were considered nomads who were little value to progressive Europe, but their significance became quite apparent when Israel arose.

The ascent of modern Arab power was made painfully clear to the industrialized world in 1973 when oil-producing Arab nations unexpectedly quadrupled the price of oil in response to Israel's victory over Egypt and Syria in the Yom Kippur War.

The world suffered economic spasms because of that decision but regardless of from which point of view we observe the Arab people, God's blessing of them through Abraham is undeniable. Abraham's other sons were esteemed to levels of importance that were previously unheard of — it was the blessing of the oil from below!

Oil became so significant that in 1991 the United States gathered the entire world against Iraq, which had invaded Kuwait. The short, one-sided war quickly extinguished the threats of Saddam Hussein's hapless army.

Arabs Desire Israel's Jerusalem

The Arabs, most of who claim to be children of Abraham, are important players in the endtimes. We will see more of that development in the days to come, as revealed in this news headline and story from *The Jerusalem Post:*

> **JERUSALEM: THE STUMBLING STONE**
>
> The Foreign Ministry has begun preliminary canvassing of all foreign embassies to see how many of them would like to

> move to Jerusalem once final status negotiations with the Palestinians are worked out, a Foreign Ministry official said."It should be clear that we are not insisting the embassies commit themselves now, but we have to begin planning for zoning purposes, and that is why we are taking this step. Municipal Boards must pass everything. We are already behind."[8]

The foreign ministry's desire to move all national embassies to "western Jerusalem" clearly indicates the government's intention to surrender parts of Jerusalem to the Arabs. It also becomes obvious that the nations want Israel to relinquish parts of Jerusalem and do the bidding of the pope who suggested the internationalization of Jerusalem in 1967.

The Jerusalem conflict is only seen in the beginning stages today and many Israeli politicians try to ignore the coming threat; however, we can see the intentions of the Palestinians from comments such as this:

> **JERUSALEM: PLO CAPITAL**
>
> Our first goal is the liberation of all occupied territories and return of all refugees, self-determination for the Palestinians and the establishment of a Palestinian state whose capital is Jerusalem. (Yasser Arafat to 19 Arab foreign ministers)[9]

Yasser Arafat and the Arab Palestinians consider all of Israel to be occupied territory. Their intention is to establish Jerusalem as the capital of a Palestinian state. While such a goal is pegged too high at this point, we must understand that part of Arafat's desire will be fulfilled. The Gaza-Jericho First move has already been implemented, and more territory will be given of Arab-Palestinians in the future.

This is the beginning of the fulfillment of prophecy described in Zechariah 12:2-3:

> Behold, I will make Jerusalem a cup of trembling unto all the people round about, when they shall be in the siege both against Judah and against Jerusalem. And in that day will I make Jerusalem a burdensome stone for all people: all that burden themselves with it shall be cut in pieces, though all the people of the earth be gathered together against it.

Final Unity

Diplomats from the United States, Europe and the United Nations cannot solve the conflict in the Middle East, nor are the Arabs capable of establishing a peace that will last. It is the Lord Himself, the Prince of Peace, who will bring about lasting peace because He paid the price for peace. He alone is able to establish reconciliation, not composed by clever politicians on a piece of paper, but based on the words: "It is finished!" These words have been sealed in His own eternally valid blood. The real price for real peace has been paid in full!

When Israel finally sees the One they pierced and recognizes Him as the Savior of the world and the

Messiah of Israel, it will not be kept hidden, but will also effect the surrounding nations. Then God will fulfill the promises He made to all of Abraham's children.

The prophet Isaiah predicted this unifying power of the Lord over 2,700 years ago:

> In that day shall there be a highway out of Egypt to Assyria, and the Assyrian shall come into Egypt, and the Egyptian into Assyria, and the Egyptians shall serve with the Assyrians. In that day shall Israel be the third with Egypt and with Assyria, even a blessing in the midst of the land. Whom the LORD of hosts shall bless, saying, Blessed be Egypt my people, and Assyria the work of my hands, and Israel mine inheritance (Isaiah 19:23-25).

In a parallel fashion, therefore, it is important that believers in the Lord Jesus Christ not allow ourselves to be deceived by the self-exalted idea that we can engineer political peace before Jesus returns. We will never be able to establish a nation or world of peace and institute Christian government in the land. It simply will not happen because God has not made any promises in Scripture to support such an idea.

CHAPTER 5

ISRAEL: THE GREATEST ENDTIME SIGN

In spite of the shocking developments that took place during the past century, the return of the Jewish people to the land of Israel and the establishment of the State of Israel are the greatest of all endtime signs, and yet the least emphasized. Israel's re-emergence as a nation is definitely a major sign of the endtimes. Israel is the only country in the Middle East with a functioning democracy. Furthermore, it is one of the freest democracies in the world. Israel's continuous progress is a barometer for global democracy.

Charles Spurgeon's Testimony

Although we have spoken about Israel several times in previous chapters, it is necessary for us to take a closer look at the re-establishment of this nation in the light of prophecy.

Servants of God who follow the Lord with all of their hearts are found few and far between, but they are the ones who recognize the future.

Charles H. Spurgeon (1834-1892) was such a person. Spurgeon taught that Israel would be a nation long before it actually happened when there appeared to be no possibility of the Jews returning to the Holy Land:

> The meaning of our text, as opened up by the context, is most evidently, if words mean anything, first, that there shall be a political restoration of the Jews to their own land and to their own nationality; and then, secondly, there is in the text, and in the context, a most plain declaration, that there shall be a spiritual restoration, a conversion in fact, of the tribes of Israel.
>
> They are to have a national prosperity which shall make them famous; nay, so glorious shall they be that Egypt, and Tyre, and Greece, and Rome, shall all forget their glory in the greater splendor of the throne of David. If there be meaning in words this must be the meaning of this chapter.
>
> I wish never to learn the art of tearing God's meaning out of His own words. If there be anything clear and plain, the literal sense and meaning of this passage — a meaning not to

> be spirited or spiritualized away — must be evident that both the two and the ten tribes of Israel are to be restored to their own land, and that a king is to rule over them.

Israel's Desire for Peace

Let us analyze the progressive development that is taking place today, which will lead Israel into union with the Europe-led New World Order. Today we see Israel mingle with its former enemies, not because the Jews have adopted a new philosophy that makes them love each other, but because of the idea of a negotiated peace.

The Jews are overwhelmed with the prospect of actually living in peace with their Arab neighbors. The Jews believe peace will come, but the Bible says just the opposite: "For when they shall say, Peace and safety; then sudden destruction cometh upon them, as travail upon a woman with child; and they shall not escape" (1 Thessalonians 5:3). This verse reveals that there will be peace and safety for Israel; thus, a negotiated peace and the resultant safety must come into being and will be the work of democracy.

After all, everyone wants peace, but how to achieve it has been the cause of many conflicts, misunderstandings and even war. We believe that the time of war is coming to a close because democracy must establish peace for the world and Israel will indeed play a leading role in that development.

At this moment the Jews, Arabs, and Islam, in conjunction with terrorism, are what most occupy the world. But those hurdles will be overcome as time goes by and peace will be established.

Israel: The Object of Prophecy

Jesus addressed the people of Israel when He identified the endtime signs that would take place before His return. Two very clear clues are mentioned in Matthew 24, which identify a certain people: "Then let them which be in Judaea flee into the mountains" (verse 16). This is a geographical reference not meant for the Church of Jesus Christ. We cannot flee to the mountains of Judea if we live anywhere but Israel.

Further, Jesus was identifying an object of prayer: "But pray ye that your flight be not in the winter, neither on the sabbath day" (verse 20). The Sabbath was given to the Jews: "Speak thou also unto the children of Israel, saying, Verily my sabbaths ye shall keep: for it is a sign between me and you throughout your generations; that ye may know that I am the LORD that doth sanctify you" (Exodus 31:13). Therefore, Israel is the great sign of the endtimes for the Gentiles and the Church!

Israel's Ancient Sin

What is Israel's goal for the future? The Jews now face their original national sin. The people of Israel were in the Promised Land almost 3,500 years ago. God had fulfilled everything He had promised concerning their entry, but Israel refused its own selection by God to be a unique nation.

God identified the deepest reason for this: the people of Israel did not want God to rule over them. They rejected God's words as conveyed to them by Moses: "For thou art an holy people unto the LORD thy God, and the LORD hath chosen thee to be a peculiar people unto himself, above all the nations that are upon the earth" (Deuteronomy 14:2).

What a tremendous promise! Israel was to be above all the nations that are upon the earth. We know from history that many nations have tried to attain this status. This elitism is obvious in America — we consider our country to be special. Most of us would even go so far as to say we live in the greatest nation in the history of the world. But many nations that existed before the United States also committed this same sin and the dust of their ruins bear witness against them.

The Holy Nation of Christians

Who are we as Christians? First Peter 2:9 answers: "But ye are a chosen generation, a royal priesthood, an holy nation, a peculiar people; that ye should shew forth the praises of him who hath called you out of darkness into his marvellous light." The Church of Jesus Christ is also a peculiar people. We are a chosen generation and a holy nation. But this holy nation is not found in any geographical or political identity.

This holy nation resides within the nations of the world and each individual member of this holy nation is known by the Lord Himself.

We have every reason to believe that this holy nation is about to be completed. When the last one from among the Gentiles has been added to the Church we will be raptured to our Lord and remain in His presence for eternity!

Israel's Request for a King

Israel's rebellious request for a king did not simply fizzle out but climaxed some 1,000 years later. We read these words in John 19:15: "We have no king but Caesar!" The full weight of their forefather's desire to be a part of the family of nations reached fruition. Israel is already being confronted with this statement as the nations of the earth gather against Jerusalem!

Someone may object to this statement because no nation, with the exception of Iran and Syria, actually has plans to fight against Jerusalem. That indeed is true, but there is something significant that many of us overlook: Jerusalem's special position in the world and in Bible prophecy. Every country on earth decides on the capital city of its country and then establishes an embassy there. Isn't it rather strange that there is no embassy in Jerusalem? Just recently the mayor of Jerusalem said, "He who rejects Jerusalem rejects Israel." This statement was made after each of the nations declined to send official representatives to celebrate Jerusalem's 40th anniversary celebration in June 2007. A spiritual reality is taking place in the invisible world, which explains why the nations oppose Jerusalem. After all, Zechariah 12:2-3 must be fulfilled: "Behold, I will make Jerusalem a cup of trembling unto all the people round about, when they shall be in the siege both against Judah and against Jerusalem. And in that day will I make Jerusalem a burdensome stone for all people: all that burden themselves with it shall be cut in pieces, though all the people of the earth be gathered together against it."

Israel's Steps Toward Peace

At this moment, it looks like the Holy Land is headed toward a negotiated peace. Increasing numbers of Israel's former enemy nations are now establishing diplomatic relationships. The possibility of increased commerce across national borders is very tempting. There's no doubt that Israel's economy will continue to grow, but all of these positive signs will never change the prophetic Word. Jesus said, "I am come in my Father's name, and ye receive me not: if another shall come in his own name, him ye will receive" (John 5:43). Israel is on its way to becoming part of the last Gentile world empire, and will ultimately accept the Antichrist.

Only when we understand these events from a spiritual aspect can we begin to comprehend what is happening in the political, economic and religious world. If we don't know the result, we may well be swallowed up by the enthusiasm created by the false peace that is being developed today, particularly through democracy.

Antichrist: The Master Deceiver

The Word of God identifies the work of the Antichrist in 2 Thessalonians 2:7-11:

> For the mystery of iniquity doth already work: only he who now letteth will let, until he be taken out of the way. And then shall that Wicked be revealed, whom the Lord shall consume with the spirit of his mouth, and shall destroy with the brightness of his coming: Even him, whose coming is after the working of Satan with all power and signs and lying wonders, And with all deceivableness of unrighteousness in them that perish; because they received not the love of the truth, that they might be saved. And for this cause God shall send them strong delusion, that they should believe a lie.

This passage of Scripture makes two things clear: the work of the Antichrist is successful through deception, and rejection of God's offer of love (John 3:16) is the cause for believing a lie.

CHAPTER 6

THE MYSTERY OF INIQUITY AND THE RAPTURE

When the Apostle Paul prophesied about the rise of the Antichrist and the last world empire, he used the term mystery of iniquity to describe a certain person whose power would have a devastating result on the entire world. The reason for calling it the mystery of iniquity shows that something is hidden, and is not generally recognized. The final revelation will only occur when the hindering element has been removed. In the meantime, we already see the beginning of the mystery of iniquity today.

Identifying the Mystery of Iniquity

The title of this chapter is found in 2 Thessalonians 2:7: "For the mystery of iniquity doth already work: only he who now letteth will let, until he be taken out of the way." The Apostle Paul made it clear that this mystery of iniquity was already at work during his time almost 2,000 years ago.

Let's look at the context in which the mystery of iniquity appears:

> Let no man deceive you by any means: for that day shall not come, except there come a falling away first, and that man of sin be revealed, the son of perdition; Who opposeth and exalteth himself above all that is called God, or that is worshipped; so that he as God sitteth in the temple of God, shewing himself that he is God. Remember ye not, that, when I was yet with you, I told you these things? And now ye know what withholdeth that he might be revealed in his time. For the mystery of iniquity doth already work: only he who now letteth will let, until he be taken out of the way. And then shall that Wicked be revealed, whom the Lord shall consume with the spirit of his mouth, and shall destroy with the brightness of his coming: Even him, whose coming is after the working of Satan with all power and signs and lying wonders, And with all deceivableness of unrighteousness in them that perish; because they received not the love of the truth, that they might be saved. And for this cause God shall send them strong delusion, that they should believe a lie: That they all might be damned who believed not the truth, but had pleasure in unrighteousness (2 Thessalonians 2:3-12).

In these few verses, we can clearly see that the mystery of iniquity, the spirit of Antichrist, was already at work at the beginning of the Church because he is a product of Satan: "Who opposeth and exalteth himself above all that is called God." Also revealed here is the removal of the Church: "until he [the Holy Spirit] be taken out of the way." Then the identification of the Antichrist will become a reality and he will be destroyed simply by the brightness of His coming.

The Great Delusion

If I could choose one word to describe these few verses it would be delusion. The work of the spirit of the Antichrist is in full swing even though the Church is still on earth. The man of sin, who receives power from Satan, produces signs and lying wonders to deceive those who received not the love of the truth.

How this deception has become a reality today was highlighted by an article in *U.S. News and World Report* (December 20, 1993). My thoughts immediately went to 1 Corinthians 1:18-25 when I read the headline of the lead story entitled, "Who was Jesus? A New Look at His Words and Deeds":

> For the preaching of the cross is to them that perish foolishness; but unto us which are saved it is the power of God. For it is written, I will destroy the wisdom of the wise, and will bring to nothing the understanding of the prudent. Where is the wise? where is the scribe? where is the disputer of this

> world? hath not God made foolish the wisdom of this world? For after that in the wisdom of God the world by wisdom knew not God, it pleased God by the foolishness of preaching to save them that believe. For the Jews require a sign, and the Greeks seek after wisdom: But we preach Christ crucified, unto the Jews a stumblingblock, and unto the Greeks foolishness; But unto them which are called, both Jews and Greeks, Christ the power of God, and the wisdom of God. Because the foolishness of God is wiser than men; and the weakness of God is stronger than men.

As I read the article, I saw how clearly it illustrated that men's wisdom is foolishness, from statements like this:

> He is depicted as an eloquent preacher and skilled healer, an exorcist and miracle worker. Now scholars are unearthing the historical truth of his life and times. Jesus proclaimed that the kingdom of God had arrived, but his view of the kingdom defied conventional wisdom.
>
> Whether or not the miracle accounts are more symbolic stories than biography, it appears to most scholars that Jesus probably did perform some miracles. "We may not be able to ascertain which miracles are authentic," says Professor Tambasco of Georgetown University. "We do have a sense that all of the stories are reworked. We can, however, be reasonably sure that all of the healings taken together witness to the fact of the miracles in the life of Jesus."[10]

All that this professor managed to do is sow additional seeds of doubt and confusion, thus typifying the great falling away because they received not the love of the truth.

Waiting for the Rapture — Not the Day of Christ

The early Christians who lived during Paul's time were waiting for the coming of the Lord but there was a misunderstanding at that time regarding the Lord's return and our gathering unto Him. Apparently someone had started spreading rumors that the Day of Christ was at hand (2 Thessalonians 2:2). These believers had become greatly troubled because the Apostle Paul had written about the Rapture in 1 Thessalonians 4:16-18, and now someone was teaching that the Day of Christ was at hand!

Paul explained that the information they received had not come from him. His concern about the issue is clearly expressed in these two verses: "Now we beseech you, brethren, by the coming of our Lord Jesus Christ, and by our gathering together unto him That ye be not soon shaken in mind, or be troubled, neither by spirit, nor by word, nor by letter as from us, as that the day of Christ is at hand" (2 Thessalonians 2:1-2).

Paul went on to describe the successive events that would occur when the actual event took place: the Church must be removed from the earth before the Antichrist is revealed.

The Removal of the Comforter

How will people be saved when the Holy Spirit is

no longer on earth? Before we answer that, let's ask a counter question: When did the Holy Spirit come? The Lord Jesus stated:

> And I will pray the Father, and he shall give you another Comforter, that he may abide with you for ever; Even the Spirit of truth; whom the world cannot receive, because it seeth him not, neither knoweth him: but ye know him; for he dwelleth with you, and shall be in you. I will not leave you comfortless: I will come to you."

This Scripture identifies the office of the Holy Spirit as being the "Comforter" (John 14:16-18). In other words, comfort will no longer be available when the Holy Spirit has departed with the Church. Those who place their faith in Jesus Christ after the Rapture and during the Great Tribulation will not be comforted with the hope of the Rapture.

Please note that the Lord specifically said, "I will not leave you comfortless: I will come to you" (John 14:18). This confirms the perfect unity we call the trinity, an established doctrine in Holy Scripture. Jesus has gone away but He is coming again through the Holy Spirit, thus, He can say, "I will come to you." The full revelation of the knowledge of the mystery of the trinity will then be revealed: "At that day ye shall know that I am in my Father, and ye in me, and I in you" (verse 20).

The Day of Christ

We learn in 2 Thessalonians 2:8 that the wicked one shall appear after the Church has been raptured. Finally, the ultimate confrontation between light and darkness will take place. The result will be the Day of Christ, when He appears in great power and glory to put an end to the Antichrist: "whom the Lord shall consume with the spirit of his mouth, and shall destroy with the brightness of his coming" (verse 8).

Comfortless Gospel

The false gospel that is being spread by some of today's theologians denies Jesus' imminent return and is actually a comfortless gospel!

The following article appeared in the May 28, 1994 edition of *The Scotsman* magazine and reveals the extent of the confusion:

> Being brought up in the Catholic religion since I was born, you can imagine how difficult it was for me to understand and accept my gift of being psychic. Christian people were always led to believe that God was above us and that the Devil was somewhere on the outside just waiting to tempt us to do wrong. It is my belief that both entities can be contained and that by the discovery of ourselves and the understanding of our motives, we can make clear choices as to what is good and what is evil. In doing so, we can determine our own spiritual path.
>
> New age thinking will allow our spirituality to grow

> much more as we leave behind the effects of Saturn, the planet that rules the churches. All religions are in for a big shakeup over the next two years, as Saturn has now entered Pisces, and I think that the religious hierarchy will need to learn how to merge and transcend, because if they don't allow a margin for alternatives their laws will become too rigid.[11]

One thing is now certain: two years have passed with no major shakeup of the world's religions. Unfortunately, such confusion is often taken seriously and people become caught up in such astrological deception.

The Strong Delusion

Scripture reveals the exact tools and avenues Satan uses to manifest his visible kingdom on earth. It is striking that God not only allows Satan's master plan for deception but He even seals it: "And for this cause God shall send them strong delusion, that they should believe a lie" (2 Thessalonians 2:11).

The true Gospel is being preached to call people to Christ and to prepare for our gathering together unto him. But God is also preparing the Day of Christ, allowing Satan's master plan of deception to be implemented: "That they all might be damned who believed not the truth, but had pleasure in unrighteousness" (verse 12). The climax of this progressive deception is accomplished by the religious aspect, which is the mystery of iniquity.

To summarize: the Day of Christ (not the Rapture, but His literal return to the Mount of Olives) cannot take place because the Antichrist has not been revealed. The revelation of the Antichrist cannot take place because the Church has not been removed from the earth.

In later chapters, we will discuss the events that lead to the final deception in greater detail.

CHAPTER 7

MYSTERY BABYLON AND ITS POWER

Who or what is Mystery Babylon? This chapter answers many controversial questions on the subject. Investigating the seven-year covenant reveals the Antichrist's success and the creation of the image of the beast, which is a technological possibility today. Mystery Babylon's intoxicating political, religious and economic fornication is dealt with in this chapter.

Mystery Babylon's Power

The term "Mystery Babylon" appears only one time in the Bible: "And upon her forehead was a name written, MYSTERY, BABYLON THE GREAT, THE MOTHER OF HARLOTS AND ABOMINATIONS OF THE EARTH" (Revelation 17:5). This is the climax of abomination, the most horrifying title anyone could possibly hold. We know that this is the epitome of evil during the endtimes as written in the book of Revelation. It is the time about which the prophets wrote centuries ago.

The Day of the Lord

To gain a clearer understanding of this terrible time, let's read how it was described by the Old Testament prophets:

"The great day of the LORD is near, it is near, and hasteth greatly, even the voice of the day of the LORD: the mighty man shall cry there bitterly. That day is a day of wrath, a day of trouble and distress, a day of wasteness and desolation, a day of darkness and gloominess, a day of clouds and thick darkness" (Zephaniah 1:14-15). Zephaniah was referring to the Day of the Lord, when Jesus returns in great power and glory to defeat the Antichrist and the entire New World Order system.

"The earth shall quake before them; the heavens shall tremble: the sun and the moon shall be dark, and the stars shall withdraw their shining: And the

LORD shall utter his voice before his army: for his camp is very great: for he is strong that executeth his word: for the day of the LORD is great and very terrible; and who can abide it?" (Joel 2:10-11).

"Alas! for that day is great, so that none is like it: it is even the time of Jacob's trouble, but he shall be saved out of it" (Jeremiah 30:7).

The Lord Jesus confirmed this prophecy when He said, "For then shall be great tribulation, such as was not since the beginning of the world to this time, no, nor ever shall be" (Matthew 24:21).

These and many other passages of Scripture identify the last part of the endtimes as the Great Tribulation.

The Seven Year Covenant

The Great Tribulation begins with the Antichrist confirming an existing covenant. Daniel 9:27 explains: "And he shall confirm the covenant with many for one week: and in the midst of the week he shall cause the sacrifice and the oblation to cease, and for the overspreading of abominations he shall make it desolate, even until the consummation, and that determined shall be poured upon the desolate."

It is important to mention that the Tribulation Period must be divided into two equal periods of 3½ years. The first half will be a time of jubilation. Those who are alive at the time will experience peace and prosperity to such a degree that the people will wholeheartedly support this New World Order that will be led by the one the Bible refers to as the Antichrist.

Antichrist's Success

The Antichrist will be very successful in his endeavors. Revelation 13:3 explains that "all the world wondered after the beast." This beast is incomparable in human history, thus, the people will ask, "Who is like unto the beast?" (Revelation 13:4). Obviously, he will also be a military genius, "who is able to make war with him?" (verse 4b).

Ultimately, the ecumenical movement, the World Council of Churches, the United Nations and whatever other group may be involved in the work towards unity, will have finally merged into one powerful religion. Thus, the Bible says, "And all that dwell upon the earth shall worship him" (verse 8).

But there is an exception. Verse 8 continues, "Whose names are not written in the book of life of the Lamb slain from the foundation of the world." The Jewish people will not participate in this one-world movement. They will be deceived by the Antichrist during the first half of the Tribulation Period, but they will not follow him during the second half. Let me explain.

Jacob's Trouble

Let's re-read Jeremiah 30:7: "Alas! for that day is

great, so that none is like it: it is even the time of Jacob's trouble; but he shall be saved out of it." Notice that the time is called Jacob's trouble. Why? I believe the reason is found in the fact that Jacob's nature was never done away with. Israel still demonstrates strong characteristics of this "Jacob" nature.

The name Jacob appears in Scripture a total of 377 times. Israel is mentioned 2,600 times. Genesis 32:28 explains that God Himself had changed Jacob's name: "And he said, Thy name shall be called no more Jacob, but Israel: for as a prince hast thou power with God and with men, and hast prevailed." This name change was later confirmed in Genesis 35:10: "Thy name shall be called no more Jacob." But a little later we read: "And God spake unto Israel in the visions of the night, and said, Jacob, Jacob. And he said, Here am I" (Genesis 46:2). Here God speaks to Israel, but He addresses him by his old name, Jacob, meaning the old flesh-and-blood Jacob, the deceiver and supplanter, was alive and well.

Such is also the case today. God has chosen Israel to reveal His intention for the entire world. The Jews have been set apart, yet the flesh-and-blood nature of Israel/Jacob prevails until this very day. That is why it is not considered Israel's trouble but Jacob's trouble. The Jacob nature, however, has been incorporated into national Israel. The Jews' desire for self-righteousness — to bring about salvation through the law — has never ceased. Thus, Israel's Jacob nature will go through a judgment period of 3 1/2 years of deception. Then a 3 1/2 year corrective period will end in the Jews' recognition of the One they had pierced followed by their salvation. Most important is to note that he (Jacob) shall be saved out of it.

Satan the Imitator

Again, we must point out that Satan is only able to imitate. Thus, in Revelation 13 the dragon gives power and authority to the beast that comes out of the sea. Verse 2b says, "And the dragon gave him his power, and his seat, and great authority." Here we see the counterfeit. The dragon offers his complete endorsement and places power and authority into the Antichrist's hands. Satan is copycatting God. The Father has given all things to the Son and Satan gives his power to the Antichrist.

Four characters that will lead the world into great deception are found in Revelation 13.

The Antichrist

"And I stood upon the sand of the sea, and saw a beast rise up out of the sea" (Revelation 13:1). We identify this beast as the Antichrist who comes from out of the sea of nations. No one really knows who he is or from where he originates. Many scholars believe he will have a Jewish background. I agree with this analysis because blessing, cursing, salvation and judgment come from Israel. Most of the men who have been and are responsible for world-changing events have been Jewish.

Satan

Satan "gave him [Antichrist, the first beast] his power, and his seat, and great authority." Satan and the Antichrist are united and both will be worshiped: "And they worshipped the dragon which gave power unto the beast: and they worshipped the beast, saying, Who is like unto the beast? who is able to make war with him?"

The False Prophet

"And I beheld another beast coming up out of the earth" (verse 11). This other beast will receive everything directly from the dragon, but the second beast already possesses power: "And he exerciseth all the power of the first beast...And deceiveth them that dwell on the earth by the means of those miracles which he had power to do in the sight of the beast...And he had power to give life unto the image of the beast" (Revelation 13:12, 14-15). We can clearly see that the second beast supports the first: "He had two horns like a lamb, and he spake as a dragon" (verse 11). He is not the Lamb of God, he is an imitation who claims to be Christ (or representative), but is not.

The Image

Finally, there is the image of the beast, which is manmade. The false prophet will initiate the creation of the image: "saying to them that dwell on the earth, that they should make an image to the beast, which had the wound by a sword, and did live" (Revelation 13:14b). In verse 15 we read that the false prophet, "had power to give life unto the image of the beast." Using a modern-day metaphor, we could say that the false prophet supplies the software for this image of the beast.

The next sentence is startling because it reveals that ultimate authority will then lie with this manmade image: "the image of the beast should both speak, and cause that as many as would not worship the image of the beast should be killed."

This manufactured image will have the capability to determine who worships it and who does not. The image will also have the authority to decide between who should live and who should die. There's no need to belabor the point that the technology exists today to produce such a deadly machine.

The following article from *Newsweek* is very convincing:

> The marriage of man (or woman) and machine is one of the most intriguing images in science fiction. From the Bionic Woman to RoboCop, these creatures are blessed with bodies that just won't quit and brains (computers) at the top of the evolutionary scale. You ain't seen nothin' yet!

> To some futurists, the most alluring possibility is what science fiction calls "wetware," the linking of the human brain and computers. The word "wet" refers to the brain; its play on hardware (computer equipment) and software (computer programs). In this vision, they would be connected directly with machines. The computer could literally read your brain waves, your thoughts — all your thoughts, mundane and majestic.
>
> Virtual telepathy is probably generations away, (if it ever happens), but researchers are currently experimenting with devices that might someday evolve into a kind of wetware. Scientists are trying to create computer images through electrodes attached to the brain, arm or facial muscles. These systems work by translating the electrical signals generated by the nervous system into patterns that computers can read. The research helps increase computer access for disabled people who could substitute a blink of an eye or the twitch of a cheek for fingers on the keyboard.[12]

Total Control

The false prophet is in obvious agreement with the dragon, who gives power to the first beast because he supports his platform on an economic, military and religious level. The false prophet will also be the great inventor of a new-world religion. Total control will be enforced for the first time in human history. When it comes to religion, the false prophet will make sure that all people will worship the image of the beast or be killed.

The Mark

The false prophet will institute a foolproof system on the financial level: "And he causeth all, both small and great, rich and poor, free and bond, to receive a mark in their right hand, or in their foreheads: And that no man might buy or sell, save he that had the mark, or the name of the beast, or the number of his name" (Revelation 13:16-17). That is total control!

In order to identify Mystery Babylon we must look for a person who is supported by a system that will exercise supreme authority in religion and economy. Let's look at the way in which our world is being changed so that such authority will not be so difficult to establish:

> There are plans on the drawing board right here in America that seems to be preparing for that day, when all must have the "mark" in order to survive, buy, sell or trade. It may not necessarily be a deliberate preparation, but we can see that it is leading in the general direction of economic control.
>
> An assigned number for every state resident would make for more efficient government, saving tax dollars, according to a proposal by a cabinet level commission. The state could have, in place, a system, that assigns every North Carolinian a computer identification number or code, that could be used to keep track of information about the person by 1997, commission members said. The commission has not ruled out using Social Security numbers. But it is not sure whether

> Federal law, which contains restrictions over the use of Social Security numbers, will allow it. The proposal could also raise fears that the state is collecting too much information about its residents, commission members said, much like the all-knowing "Big Brother" in George Orwell's novel, 1984.[13]

Control Welcomed

In order to better understand what has been predicted in Scripture, we must not look at all things in the modern world from a negative point of view. Surely every upstanding citizen supports the elimination of crime. Proper electronic control could virtually eliminate the drug trade.

We must also consider the many billions of dollars the IRS is unable to collect due to insufficient control. The greater this system of control is developed and refined, the broader the support it will receive from the public. The implementation of a new and efficient tax collection method may result in lower rates.

Political Babylon

Mystery Babylon is referred to as a woman, but is later identified as a city, "And the woman which thou sawest is that great city, which reigneth over the kings of the earth" (Revelation 17:18). We learn from this verse that Mystery Babylon possesses religious and economic authority as well as political power; otherwise the "kings" of the earth, the political leaders, would not have anything to do with her.

Fornication

Also worth mentioning here is that Mystery Babylon commits fornication. Therefore, it is evident that this woman/city has some political dealings with presidents, prime ministers, dictators and kings, the financial elite and world religion. Fornication is the product of this union between the woman/city and the kings of the earth; thus, she is not only referred to as a whore, but "the great whore."

The word "fornication" is repeated 36 times in Scripture, primarily to identify illicit sexual relationships. In regard to Mystery Babylon, however, the word is mentioned eight times in relation to prosperity. For example, "For all nations have drunk of the wine of the wrath of her fornication, and the kings of the earth have committed fornication with her, and the merchants of the earth are waxed rich through the abundance of her delicacies" (Revelation 18:3).

Worldwide Fornication

This fornication applies not only to the rulers (kings) of this earth, but to all people in the world. Wine is the substance that people will use to participate in this fornication. The result is revealed in verse 2: they "have been made drunk with the wine of her fornication." This is not some local matter where fornication is committed with a king or two, but the text explicitly points an accusing finger at the "kings of the earth" — all of them.

Mystery Babylon is so powerful that the rulers will have to deal with her in order to participate in this successful one-world system. And the great whore will intoxicate the people of the earth with religious, political, and economic success.

The establishment of these facts makes it clear that there is only one legitimate political system: democracy!

Worldwide Communication

Effective global communication was impossible only a century ago. At that time communication was limited to transportation. Ships, horse and buggies, and the introduction of the steam engine were the main methods of transportation. Operating a system that includes all people must have the capability to instantly communicate globally. Today, satellites allow for instantaneous global communication, and one can travel by jet to any place in the world, sometimes even faster than the speed of sound.

With the advancement of computer technology, there is often no need to even travel. Teleconferencing has become an extremely popular trend — business can be conducted without leaving your office. That means a truly worldwide system — a former impossibility — has become a reality!

Intoxicated Babylon

It is both illegal and dangerous to drive while intoxicated; nevertheless, there are people that get in the driver seat after a night of drinking and believe that they have sufficient command of their abilities. They do not consider the danger their decision to drive presents to them or to the other drivers. Naturally the person was able to safely operate the vehicle before he started drinking, but now that he is drunk, his judgment and physical ability has become impaired, nonetheless, he becomes overly confident and tragedy often follows.

We don't have to be experts to see that the world is already intoxicated with the "wine" of the "fornication" of "the great whore" to such an extent that people actually believe all problems can be solved by their own initiatives.

Intoxicating Democracy

Is there anyone who does not believe that democracy, the system in which people rule themselves, is the best of all political philosophies? Is there any political institution or center of higher learning that realizes we cannot help ourselves or solve the problems of our world outside of God?

Representatives of every political system believe they have the ability to solve all the world's problems. Today, for the first time in history, people believe that democracy is the savior of the world.

Intoxicating Education

Walk into a college or university and propose to

our students that they must obey the God who created heaven and earth so that they might understand who they are and what their purpose is on this earth. You can bet that the majority of students and teachers would mock us for making such a suggestion. Man has already become spiritually drunk and does not know who he is, where he is going, or what his future will be like.

What would a professor from Harvard say if you told him or her the biblical truth about man's condition? "But we are all as an unclean thing, and all our righteousnesses are as filthy rags; and we all do fade as a leaf; and our iniquities, like the wind, have taken us away" (Isaiah 64:6). They would probably question your mental state after dismissing such a statement as nonsense.

Self Love: Babylon

It is no longer acceptable in the religious world to teach that man is corrupt, lost, unable to help himself, and on his way to eternal damnation. Unfortunately the same can also be said within Christianity. Only a few would accept that "we are all as an unclean thing, and all our righteousnesses are as filthy rags." That idea is contrary to what the world teaches and also professing Christianity at large. In fact, today's society (made drunk with the wine of the whore's self-image) is being taught to over-emphasize man's nobility, to think positive, and to do everything in his power to build up a person's self-esteem.

We are being told that the reason our prisons are filled to overflowing and lawlessness is running rampant is not because of sin, but it is because of the prisoner's upbringing, his surroundings, or circumstances such as economic deprivation. Criminals who fill our prisons are being taught that if they can learn to love themselves and understand that their low self-esteem and low self-worth were responsible for their actions, then they can re-enter society as a rehabilitated individual.

Most people actually believe that sinful and corrupt men can be changed by proper analysis of self and through behavior modification programs. Words such as prisons, inmates, convicts, and the like are no longer politically correct. A criminal in prison becomes a resident of a correctional institution.

Is it necessary to point out that the world is intoxicated by its fornication with Mystery Babylon? Do we need any more proof? Obviously not!

According to numerous reports, self-love is the very reason for criminal behavior. The following is an article from Creation Moments:

> **"Studies Link Violence with Self-Love"**
>
> Popular psychology has for years declared that troubled young people, especially those who become violent, suffer

from low self-esteem. But three studies released in the summer of 1999 conclude the opposite: young people, who become violent, have too much self-esteem.

One of the studies published by the American Psychological Association, observed 540 undergraduate students. After answering standard questions designed to measure self-esteem and narcissism, the students were put into different situations. They were given the opportunity to act aggressively against someone who had praised them, insulted them or did nothing to them. Researchers found that the most narcissistic students were the most likely to react violently. They also found that narcissists were especially aggressive against anyone who had offended them. Another study found narcissism is prevalent among prisoners convicted of rape, murder, assault, armed robbery and similar crimes. When their self-esteem was measured against the general population, it was found to be above average. The researchers involved in this study pointed out that the primary focus of prison rehabilitation is on building self-esteem. This, they concluded, is definitely the wrong approach, since such people already have an inflated view of themselves.

Christian Babylon

Most shocking, however, is that this intoxication is having an effect on born-again Bible-believers. Biblical counseling is no longer considered the proper way to solve a personality conflict. Today, people are being sent to Christian psychologists or psychiatrists. Woe unto the pastor who tells a person to repent of his or her sins!

Our judicial system no longer accepts the spiritual authority of a church leader, yet a so-called properly trained counselor with earned degrees in psychology or psychiatry is now deemed as qualified to analyze a person with a problem and prescribe the proper remedy.

Psychology Repairs — Jesus Renews

There's no doubt that psychology, psychiatry, and other types of unbiblical counseling are helpful. We cannot deny the success of many Christian psychologists who have taught countless people how to deal with their problems. After all, a good talk with a trained psychologist may do wonders for a person, but so could a good talk with anyone else.

Some Buddhists, Hindus, and Muslims also seek counsel from therapists. The truth, however, is that when you come to Jesus and wholeheartedly confess your sins to Him and repent of them, you will not just be helped, but you will be liberated from them! The psychologist may repair, but Jesus renews! The Bible says, "If the Son therefore shall make you free, ye shall be free indeed" (John 8:36).

Jesus Liberates

Of course, you can be freed, for example, from the habit of smoking. Hundreds of avenues provide methods to break the habit. You can even sign up for a program that hospitalizes a person and provides medical assistance to free you of the addiction. But what's wrong with simply asking Jesus to help you break the habit? Why not tell Jesus that you want to be free of the addiction of nicotine, free from impure thoughts, free from lying, free from gossiping? Simply get down on your knees, repent of that sin, and thank Him that He has cleansed you with His own precious blood. He has already paid the price for your sins, and you can receive total liberty from any oppression or depression. You can be free right this minute!

The Word of God is eternally valid, but we must be willing to come to the light. The Bible says, "But if we walk in the light, as he is in the light, we have fellowship one with another, and the blood of Jesus Christ his Son cleanseth us from all sin" (1 John 1:7). This verse does not say from certain sins for a limited time but from all sins. Verse 9 provides the absolute guarantee: "If we confess our sins, he is faithful and just to forgive us our sins, and to cleanse us from all unrighteousness."

CHAPTER 8

MYSTERY BABYLON IDENTIFIED

The Bible clearly mentions two entities in relation to the identity of Mystery Babylon: a city and a whore. Religious deception and political democracy are shown in their proper relationship to the fulfillment of end-time Bible prophecy. A four-fold criterion identifies Mystery Babylon. We also learn how the Roman system, through Europe, will unify this world politically, economically and religiously. The process is underway today.

Mystery Babylon Identified

The Apostle John, who actually saw Mystery Babylon, was completely surprised. One translation says he "was astonished with great astonishment." What John saw was inconceivable. He came face to face with the endtime climax of evil: "the mother of harlots and abominations of the earth" (verse 5). John witnessed more details than Daniel had seen more than five centuries earlier!

There is a four-fold criterion that helps us to identify Mystery Babylon.

1) The martyrs of Jesus: "And I saw the woman drunken with the blood of the saints, and with the blood of the martyrs of Jesus: and when I saw her, I wondered with great admiration" (Revelation 17:6). Surely there is no other city in the world where the blood of the martyrs of Jesus was shed more so than in Rome. Christian persecution became a national sport. Huge crowds cheered as lions ripped Christian men, women and children to shreds.

Daniel Saw Mystery Babylon

In Daniel's case, we read of the last world empire: "After this I saw in the night visions, and behold a fourth beast, dreadful and terrible, and strong exceedingly; and it had great iron teeth: it devoured and brake in pieces, and stamped the residue with the feet of it: and it was diverse from all the beasts that were before it; and it had ten horns" (Daniel 7:7).

Daniel was astonished. He inquired about this fourth beast in verse 19: "Then I would know the truth of the fourth beast, which was diverse from all the others, exceeding dreadful."

He received the answer in verse 23: "The fourth beast shall be the fourth kingdom upon earth, which shall be diverse from all kingdoms, and shall devour the whole earth, and shall tread it down, and break it in pieces."

John saw additional details but he, too, had a problem and expressed his need for help: "And the angel said unto me, Wherefore didst thou marvel? I will tell thee the mystery of the woman, and of the beast that carrieth her, which hath the seven heads and ten horns" (Revelation 17:7). Two identities are being revealed: a woman and a beast. Now comes the explanation beginning in verse 8: "The beast that thou sawest was, and is not; and shall ascend out of the bottomless pit, and go into perdition: and they that dwell on the earth shall wonder, whose names were not written in the book of life from the foundation of the world, when they behold the beast that was, and is not, and yet is."

It's important to point out that John saw the future in the form of the present. He was in heaven in the spirit, "Come up hither." Revelation 4:2 says, "Immediately, I was in the spirit." Subsequently, John could describe these events from a heavenly perspective.

He confirmed that all the earth would wonder after the beast. One translation of the Greek word "wonder" in Revelation 13:13 is that all the world will be so astounded that they will literally be driven insane by this beast!

A modern analogy would be the pandemonium that breaks out when a rock group takes the stage. Tens of thousands of people go wild; actually go out of character, as their heroes strut out before them. Each individual becomes one with the sea of humanity glorifying the rock idols as the music begins.

2) Seven hills: The second sign of identification is found in Revelation 17:9: "And here is the mind which hath wisdom. The seven heads are seven mountains, on which the woman sitteth." We learn from verse 18 that the woman is a city, "And the woman which thou sawest is that great city, which reigneth over the kings of the earth." Thus, Mystery Babylon must be a geographically identifiable city that is built upon seven hills. Rome is built upon seven hills.

Furthermore, the angel does not fail to stress that world unity is a coming reality in conjunction with this city: "These have one mind, and shall give their power and strength unto the beast" (verse 13). Verse 15 explains verse 1 regarding the woman sitting upon many waters: "And he saith unto me, The waters which thou sawest, where the whore sitteth, are peoples, and multitudes, and nations, and tongues." This verse reinforces the interpretation that the last world system, which originates with Rome, will rule over the nations.

3) Kings of the earth: We must first read Revelation 18:3 in order to determine the third criteria: "For all nations have drunk of the wine of the wrath of her fornication, and the kings of the earth have committed fornication with her, and the merchants of the earth are waxed rich through the abundance of her delicacies."

No other city in the world can claim to have a special relationship with global political leaders, yet be strictly religious in nature — Rome is the only contender!

Daniel Confirms

A strong economy will be created as a result of this fornicating relationship among global political leaders that will make the people on earth very wealthy. Daniel confirmed this prophetically:

> And in the latter time of their kingdom, when the transgressors are come to the full, a king of fierce countenance, and understanding dark sentences, shall stand up. And his power shall be mighty, but not by his own power: and he shall destroy wonderfully, and shall prosper, and practise, and shall destroy the mighty and the holy people. And through his policy also he shall cause craft to prosper in his hand; and he shall magnify himself in his heart, and by peace shall destroy many:

> he shall also stand up against the Prince of princes; but he shall be broken without hand (Daniel 8:23-25).

The books of Daniel and Revelation allow us to see how this new but final world empire is being established. Geographically, it originates in a city that is built upon seven hills, in which the blood of the martyrs of Jesus was shed, and out of which shall emerge a man who will be extremely successful.

Occult Deception

Daniel described a king who would possess the unique ability to understand dark sentences. This describes the occult. Daniel also revealed the secret of his understanding: the power will not be the king's, but it will be given to him by the dragon (Revelation 13). This man will do great and mighty things and shall prosper. Martin Luther translates this verse as follows: "Through his wisdom, he shall be successful with his deception." No doubt, he will be the most successful man on earth, but when he reaches that point of success, he will make a fatal mistake: he will allow pride to take hold of him to such an extent that he will literally declare war against the God of heaven!

4) A city on fire that can be seen from the Mediterranean Sea: The fourth sign of identification is found in Revelation 18. God remembers her iniquity, "and she shall be utterly burned with fire" (verse

8) after "her sins have reached unto heaven" (verse 5). When that happens, we see that the kings of the earth (the political elite), the merchants of the earth (the economic system), and "all the company in ships, and sailors, and as many as trade by sea, stood afar off" (verse 17) "cried when they saw the smoke of her burning, saying, What city is like unto this great city!" (verse 18). That means the entire world will be rocked by Mystery Babylon's destruction, and the smoke that rises from this city will be visible from the Mediterranean Sea.

Only Rome Qualifies

To summarize: the city must meet the following qualifications before it can be crowned Mystery Babylon — it must be responsible for shedding the blood of the martyrs of Jesus, it must be located upon seven hills, it must commit political/religious fornication with the leaders of the world, and it must also be visible from the sea when on fire. There is no other city that can fit this four-fold criterion.

Rome is the only city in the world that contains a recognized nation: the Vatican. Many people fail to understand that the Vatican, the headquarters of the Catholic Church, is not only a religious organization, but also an established political state recognized by virtually all nations, including the United Nations. As a matter of fact, the Vatican has diplomatic relations with more nations than the United States.

Rome's Success

For example, the United States is an overwhelmingly Protestant country, yet each of its presidents has been received by the pope for an audience. Surely if the leaders of both nations were equal, then they could meet on equal ground but such is not the case with the pope of Rome. An audience is granted to a subject, which is lower than the one giving the audience. Thereby, the leaders of the United States have literally committed fornication with this religious/political figurehead, who claims to be the only legitimate representative of Christ on earth — a blatant contradiction to Scripture.

Catholicism presents a great problem for fundamental Bible believers and vice-versa. A newspaper article explains this struggle:

> A new Vatican document on how to interpret the Bible condemns the fundamentalist approach as distorting and possibly leading to racism. The 130-page document… is the Roman Catholic Church's latest commentary on trends in Biblical study. Some of its language is unusually harsh, reflecting the challenge that fundamentalists pose to the church.
>
> "Without saying as much, in so many words, fundamentalism actually invites people to intellectual suicide," says the document from the Pontifical Biblical Commission. The authors save their harshest language for Christian fundamentalist denominations, which have been posing a chal-

> lenge to the Roman church, particularly in Latin America...
> "The fundamentalist approach is dangerous, for it is attractive to people who look to the Bible for ready answers to the problems of life."[14]

Rome vs. Scripture

This article was printed in our daily newspaper and reveals the effectiveness of Bible-believing missionary activity. The negative tone the author has used regarding Christian fundamentalists reveals the Vatican's fear of losing its stranglehold on hundreds of millions of people who are being led astray by such false doctrines as the pope's infallibility, purgatory, the Eucharist, the rosary, worship of the dead, worship of Mary, plus other extra-biblical activities that are contrary to the precious Word of God.

Vatican doctrine, at the zenith of its visible wickedness, led to the sale of indulgences; that is, the forgiveness of sins through the payment of money to the Roman treasury.

Yes, indeed, the fundamentalist (Bible) approach is dangerous to the Vatican, because it can liberate lost souls from the bondage of a man-made religion and lead them to liberty in Jesus Christ through the preaching of the Gospel.

Rome Uniting Religions

We also know about the activity of Pope John Paul II regarding the union of all religions. The goal has not been just to have all Protestant churches unite under the World Council of Churches and then under the Roman Catholic Church but the intention goes much further to actually striving to unify ALL of the world's religions under the Roman umbrella. All nations and religions must be melded into one in order to fulfill biblical prophecy, "And all that dwell upon the earth shall worship him" (Revelation 13:8). *In Global Peace and the Rise of Antichrist,* Dave Hunt wote:

> The entire May/June 1988 issue of *The Catholic World* was devoted to Buddhism. The articles were all sympathetic, including favorable quotes from the pope. One article was even titled "The Buddha Revered As A Christian Saint"! John Paul II takes a broad-minded view of Buddhism and all other religions. He considers the Tibetan Buddhist Deity Yoga of his good friend the Dalai Lama, along with the prayers of witch doctors, spiritists, and every other "faith" to be generating profound spiritual energies that are creating a new climate of peace.
>
> ... Pope John Paul II slipped off his shoes to sit quietly and solemnly with the supreme patriarch of Thailand's Buddhists at a Buddhist monastery in Bangkok.... The Roman Catholic pontiff later praised the ancient and venerable wisdom of the Asian religion.[15]

Unifying Power of Babylon

Mystery Babylon is the religious power of the last world empire that can be realized for the first time in history. It is not a power that is based on brutal, oppressive military force; it is a system that is supported by people the world over.

No one can deny that democracy has become the god of politics. Woe unto any leader that refuses to implement democracy in his or her nation. While there are still rebels here and there, it will ultimately become impossible to withstand this new democratic world power structure that is even now beginning to sweep the world. The United Nations is already punishing the leaders of many nations for not implementing democracy.

For example, it was impossible for the United States to reject NAFTA [North American Free Trade Agreement] or the GATT [General Agreement on Tariffs and Trade] treaties. These and other trade agreements that follow are only part of the process that will lead the world into a virtually perfect union. Finally, men will believe that they have achieved — with their own power and free will — unprecedented peace, stability, and prosperity.

People will not need to be forced to worship, praise, and wonder after the beast; they will voluntarily want to participate in this New World Order and will enthusiastically worship the beast and his image.

Worldwide Babylon

The power of Mystery Babylon, although spiritually headquartered in Rome, will not be isolated to that geographical city, it will be worldwide. When we look at European history, we notice that only Europe has affected the entire world. The Chinese did not go to Africa and establish colonies nor did the Africans go to America and conquer land. Only Europe was able to subdue virtually the entire world, because of the power of the Roman system.

After many wars — especially two world wars — Europe has learned that unity will not be achieved through weapons. Thus, we saw the determined progress being made towards a unified Europe by means of political and financial policy. While it seemed like a utopian dream not many years ago, that is no longer the case today. The European Union is such a reality that the question of its existence is no longer valid. The big question today is this: When will more nations be accepted into the European Union? The more the Union grows, the more the nations will try to become a part of it.

Ten Horns and Kings

We have dealt with Revelation 13, the Antichrist, Satan, the false prophet, and the image of the beast, but now it seems necessary to mention an often misunderstood verse in which Daniel also wrote: the beast "having seven heads and ten horns, and upon his horns ten crowns" (verse 1).

According to my understanding of the prophetic Word, I believe that the ten horns, which are ten kings, mentioned in Revelation 17:12 — do not represent ten European nations, but rather ten different demonic power structures. It is unrealistic to assume that North America, for example, would become a full-fledged member of the European Union because of its geographic location. Therefore, an allied power structure will be established in various parts of the world, but it will be formed under the leadership of the European Union.

In the same way the Roman European civilization has conquered the world, the new system now being established will equally conquer the world, not by military force, but rather through a political, religious and economic system that will be superior to all others.

Someone may now ask: Did Europe really conquer the world? My answer would be absolutely yes! There is no question about Europe and European-cultured continents such as America and Australia, but Africa and Asia must also follow in the footsteps of Roman civilization in order to compete in a modern world. China has no chance of becoming part of the world's economy unless it acts "European"; that is, to dress, communicate, and govern according to the Roman model. For example, you don't ever see an African involved in a business transaction, using his own cultural methods. The entire political/economic system is based on the European Roman model.

Europe Will Lead

Some may still doubt that the New World Order now being established through the European Union will rule the world but I am convinced that there will no longer be any doubt in a few years. It is evident, at least on the financial level, that Europe has surpassed the United States. America can no longer dictate the financial and economic structure of the world as it has in days past.

Such developments, however, are necessary for the fulfillment of the prophetic Word — not only Europe, but the entire world must follow the pattern of the European Roman civilization. Even China, the world's most populated nation, which is presently ruled by the communist system, is slowly but surely patterning itself after the European Roman system. The following news article reveals how China is on the road to Rome:

> Persistence pays.
>
> That's what the European Union is finding in negotiations with Asia.
>
> Almost 10 months of painstaking negotiations have resolved a long-standing conflict over China's $2 billion in silk, linen and exports to the E.U. market.
>
> Big increases in import quotas by the E.U. have mollified the Chinese and muted protests by European importers.
>
> At the same time, the E.U. won Chinese agreement to cooperate on new E.U.-wide restrictions.

> Officials say all three agreements concluded on January 20 — covering almost $9-billion worth of E.U. trade in textiles and clothing — were thrashed out without too much acrimony. It was a question of persistence rather than threats, says an E.U. trade official.[16]

We have witnessed near breathtaking changes between Europe and the United States during the last four decades. There was no question in anyone's mind regarding America's superiority after World War II but that is no longer true today. America has become increasingly more dependent upon Europe. That is the progressive fulfillment of Bible prophecy, which documents that all nations will unite through the "fornicating power" of the European system, identified in Scripture as Mystery Babylon.

Final Rebellion

What, then, is the real purpose of Mystery Babylon? It is the final rebellion of satanic forces against the living God and His Anointed. Psalm 2 makes this very clear: "Why do the heathen rage, and the people imagine a vain thing? The kings of the earth set themselves, and the rulers take counsel together, against the LORD, and against his anointed, saying, Let us break their bands asunder, and cast away their cords from us" (Psalm 2:1-3). This is precisely what is beginning to happen: the world is coming together, not necessarily for the purpose of destroying communism, dictatorship, or some other system but it is ultimately to oppose the Creator of heaven and earth. People will say no to His Son, the Anointed One, in through whom there is eternal salvation, genuine peace and prosperity.

In this drunken state, the people do not sense the intoxication, but they will continue to protest and build upon their own sin-tainted imaginations.

The unity of the world under the Antichrist will become so strong that they will have the courage to actually wage war against the Lamb: "These shall make war with the Lamb, and the Lamb shall overcome them: for he is Lord of lords, and King of kings: and they that are with him are called, and chosen, and faithful" (Revelation 17:14).

Avoiding the Deception that Will Sweep the World

Mystery Babylon is being revealed progressively today. Only those who keep themselves pure through the Lord Jesus Christ are able to see and understand that the Lord is about to return for His Church. The full potency of evil will be revealed the moment the Church of Jesus Christ has been raptured.

Jesus said, "Ye are the light of the world." The Church is the hindering element for the full development of rebellion. Darkness and deception will prevail on earth the moment this "light" is taken out of the way, and then the devil can finally implement his full intention. Believers are not ignorant of Satan's devices, and that is one more reason we should continuously study the Holy Word of God regarding future events.

I must stress that this evil is being presented in such a positive way that if it were possible, even the elect would be deceived. The power of Mystery Babylon is deception: "for by thy sorceries were all nations deceived" (Revelation 18:23). Christians who believe in the Word of God know how the story ends, and we rejoice in that which is to come: "Therefore rejoice, ye heavens, and ye that dwell in them. Woe to the inhabiters of the earth and of the sea! for the devil is come down unto you, having great wrath, because he knoweth that he hath but a short time" (Revelation 12:12).

CHAPTER 9

EUROPE IN PROPHECY

The amazing manifestation of the Roman Empire is being made visible through the formation of the European Union. This chapter shows how previously successful nations will become subject to the new political, economic, and religious power structure of the European Union. Europe, the world's smallest continent, is the only one that meets the Bible's specifications as being the last Gentile power structure in fulfillment of Daniel 7:23: "Thus he said, The fourth beast shall be the fourth kingdom upon earth, which shall be diverse from all kingdoms, and shall devour the whole earth, and shall tread it down, and break it in pieces."

Europe in Prophecy

Why can't we say "America in Prophecy" or "Africa in Prophecy?" The answer is simple: the Bible concerns itself primarily with the return of the Messiah to Israel. Therefore, the focal point of Bible prophecy is the nations that surround Israel and their relationship to the land. Israel is the center of three continents — Europe, Asia, and Africa. Asia is mentioned several times in Scripture, as are a number of African countries such as Ethiopia, Egypt, Libya, etc.

Egypt, for example, is significant because it is there that Israel became a nation and from which the children of Israel departed 430 years later where they set out for the Promised Land. It was in Egypt that the Lord Jesus was protected from the wrath of King Herod.

But what about the great Turkish Empire that ruled the entire Middle East? Or Britain? It was said that the sun never set on the British Empire. Surely the United States can be considered a world power structure that has left a significant mark on the planet. Many other nations have also achieved mighty things. Nevertheless, these and other nations are not mentioned in relationship to Israel because they did not exist during the time of Jesus' First Coming, nor did they demonstrate any major significance during the time of Christ on earth.

Rome was the center of political, economic and military activity during the time of Christ. The power of the Roman Empire had spread across most of what we know today as Europe, including all of the Mediterranean countries.

Four Gentile Empires

This is why we can legitimately focus on Europe's role in Bible prophecy. While history records the mighty deeds of a number of different nations, the Bible recognizes only four Gentile power structures throughout history: Babylon, Medo-Persia, Greece, and Rome. Therefore, we must not allow our focus to become distracted from the main geographic location on earth — Israel, and the greatest of all power structures, Europe. Also, we do well to remember that America, most of Africa, and Australia are political realities because of Europe's power.

Daniel's View

The prophet Daniel has provided a remarkable view of the four Gentile power structures. He was a captive in Babylon and yearned to be home in Israel. Surely his heart went out to Jerusalem and the temple, which had been destroyed during his time. But God used Daniel in a foreign land to show us the power structure of the Gentile nations from beginning to end.

Babylon

King Nebuchadnezzar was the ruler of Babylon,

the first Gentile world empire mentioned in the Bible. The unfolding of the prophetic Word begins with his dream. Nebuchadnezzar could not recall the details of his dream when he awoke. He immediately called upon his intelligence advisors, the prognosticators, and the think-tank of that time: "Then the king commanded to call the magicians, and the astrologers, and the sorcerers, and the Chaldeans, for to shew the king his dreams. So they came and stood before the king" (Daniel 2:2).

After they heard that the king had a dream, they confessed that they were powerless to describe or interpret it: "And it is a rare thing that the king requireth, and there is none other that can shew it before the king, except the gods, whose dwelling is not with flesh" (Daniel 2:11).

This is also true today. Politicians, intellectuals, leaders of the world, and the news media are in total darkness when it comes to knowing the future; therefore, we must consult Him who holds the future in His hand and invites us to, "Ask [Him] of things to come" (Isaiah 45:11).

Nebuchadnezzar's Dream

No one was able to describe the details of the king's dream; subsequently, no one could interpret it. Then Nebuchadnezzar summoned a young Jewish man named Daniel who said to the king:

> Thou, O king, sawest, and behold a great image. This great image, whose brightness was excellent, stood before thee; and the form thereof was terrible. This image's head was of fine

> gold, his breast and his arms of silver, his belly and his thighs of brass, His legs of iron, his feet part of iron and part of clay. Thou sawest till that a stone was cut out without hands, which smote the image upon his feet that were of iron and clay, and brake them to pieces. Then was the iron, the clay, the brass, the silver, and the gold, broken to pieces together, and became like the chaff of the summer threshingfloors; and the wind carried them away, that no place was found for them: and the stone that smote the image became a great mountain, and filled the whole earth (Daniel 2:31-35).

How Europe is Emerging to Assume Leadership

Destruction is the result of the nations' power structure. No nation, regardless of how great or small, has a future on its own merits. Not even the revived Roman Empire ultimately has a positive future, but Daniel prophesied that Rome will be a major power structure with links to Israel.

Officials in the Israeli government have in recent years praised the European Union, and expressed hopes that it will play a significant role in the peace process. Consider the following comments made by former Israeli Prime Minister Shimon Peres:

> "I believe that the role of EC in restructuring the new Middle East is major and essential," he said during a press conference with European President Jacques Delors. The

> European Community has pledged hundreds of millions of dollars of aid for Palestinians if Israel will relinquish territory in the West Bank, Gaza and Golan Heights.[17]

With this statement, Peres exposed the Union's intention to the world: surrender Promised Land territory in exchange for negotiated peace.

Gold, Silver, Brass and Iron

Daniel interpreted Nebuchadnezzar's dream:

> Thou, O king, art a king of kings: for the God of heaven hath given thee a kingdom, power, and strength, and glory. And wheresoever the children of men dwell, the beasts of the field and the fowls of the heaven hath he given into thine hand, and hath made thee ruler over them all. Thou art this head of gold. And after thee shall arise another kingdom inferior to thee, and another third kingdom of brass, which shall bear rule over all the earth. And the fourth kingdom shall be strong as iron: forasmuch as iron breaketh in pieces and subdueth all things: and as iron that breaketh all these, shall it break in pieces and bruise. And whereas thou sawest the feet and toes, part of potters' clay, and part of iron, the kingdom shall be divided; but there shall be in it of the strength of the iron, forasmuch as thou sawest the iron mixed with miry clay. And as the toes of the feet were part of iron, and part of clay, so the kingdom shall be partly strong, and partly broken. And whereas thou sawest iron mixed with miry

> clay, they shall mingle themselves with the seed of men: but they shall not cleave one to another, even as iron is not mixed with clay. And in the days of these kings shall the God of heaven set up a kingdom, which shall never be destroyed: and the kingdom shall not be left to other people, but it shall break in pieces and consume all these kingdoms, and it shall stand for ever. Forasmuch as thou sawest that the stone was cut out of the mountain without hands, and that it brake in pieces the iron, the brass, the clay, the silver, and the gold; the great God hath made known to the king what shall come to pass hereafter: and the dream is certain, and the interpretation thereof sure (Daniel 2:37-45).

We notice that the description does not begin with the feet and move upward but vice-versa. In other words, the best is first and the worst is last: "Thou, O king, art a king of kings... Thou art this head of gold" (verses 37-38). Thus, Nebuchadnezzar's superiority is evident by the components of this image: 1) gold, 2) silver, 3) brass, and 4) iron and clay. These four empires are clearly identified and there is no question among Bible scholars regarding who they represent:

Gold — Babylon
Silver — Medo-Persia
Brass — Greece
Iron — Rome

Daniel wrote more about the iron empire than he did about the other three combined.

The Mystery of the Iron and Clay

Also significant is that a fifth component, clay, is added, but this clay was not part of the iron empire from the beginning. The clay and iron mixture is found only in the feet and toes. Although this is one empire, there is definitely a significant change in the end: the beginning of the fourth empire was iron and the Pax Romani policy was based on military superiority. The last part of this empire still possesses its military strength of iron but clay is also added. What does the clay symbolize? I believe the clay represents the Jewish people.

Dictatorship vs. Democracy

When we compare this last empire to the previous ones, we must admit that the iron/clay mixture is extremely poor quality. Actually, the two don't mix well at all.

Gold is a precious commodity, but iron is available in abundance. Clay is even more available than iron. These matters are shocking because for the most part people will reject, even condemn dictatorship and praise our system of democracy. But in the spirit of democracy, the king of Babylon would be described as a brutal dictator under whom the people suffered greatly. In contrast, democracy is considered the liberty of mankind. We think highly of democracy because "we the people" are in charge. We vote leaders into office who will rule us according to our laws, which we have coined according to our preferences. This type of government could not have come into being during the Roman Empire because democracy was reserved for the upper class. They still ruled their own land and those they had conquered with a rod of iron.

Communism and the Jews

The first major change took place in 1848 when Karl Marx and Frederick Engels published *The Communist Manifesto*. Not surprisingly, the Jews were the first to promote this system because it promised them equality. This was the first major attempt in modern times for the Jews to be integrated into the family of Gentiles. Later, communism was taken over by an elite, anti-Semitic leadership, which resulted in severe persecution of the Jews; thus, they experienced oppression instead of liberty.

Communism: Anti-Religion

A major reason for communism was that the Jews were a religious people whether they admitted it or not. Communists rejected religion and called it the "opium of the people." Thus, the Jewish drive for freedom and equality developed more successfully in the new world, primarily in the United States. Religious freedom was guaranteed and democracy was not only in the stage of being established in the United States but was often exported to other nations. Democracy eventually became a death sentence for communism.

Democracy Rules

There is no longer a question over which system is superior — it is democracy. We are witnessing the uniting of the world under the democratic umbrella. This union is absolutely necessary in order to fulfill Bible prophecy: "These have one mind" (Revelation 17:13). Men are working feverishly to communicate better in order to facilitate this like-minded union.

An article in *Popular Science* magazine reveals how men want to reverse the effect of the Tower of Babel:

> **Reversal of the Tower of Babel**
>
> Once a language interpreter and now a computer scientist, Hiraaki Kitano dreams of a machine that combines elements of both disciplines: A handheld computer and speech translator that could knock down the language barriers once and for all. Speak English words into the computer, for example, and out will come the same words spoken aloud in Spanish, French, or Japanese.
>
> While electronic translators exist in limited form today, none of them use the kind of highly sophisticated voice-recognition and text-to-speech technology that would be needed to perform real-time bilingual exchanges quickly and accurately. At Carnegie Mellon University in Pittsburgh, Kitano is using a supercomputer and a separate device for voice recognition and voice synthesis to develop a new speech-to-speech translating system.[18]

There is no doubt that men will eradicate the effect in which the Tower of Babel had on society: the genesis of many different languages. The Lord confused the former one-world language in order to separate the various tribes of people. Genesis 11:6 reads: "And the LORD said, Behold, the people is one, and they have all one language; and this they begin to do: and now nothing will be restrained from them, which they have imagined to do."

The development toward a one-world language does not need to be a language by itself, but rather an elimination of the hindrances to understanding each other. Eventually it will come about by this new speech-to-speech system employing artificial intelligence software.

Lion, Bear, Leopard — Dreadful and Terrible

As we mentioned, the last kingdom is an extension of the fourth kingdom, but is slightly different. The iron-clay kingdom is definitely diverse. It has different characteristics, and is the only government that mixes two components.

In Daniel 7 the prophet passes on additional information he received to reinforce that the final kingdom will be different from all the others:

> Daniel spake and said, I saw in my vision by night, and, behold, the four winds of the heaven strove upon the great sea. And four great beasts came up from the sea, diverse one

> from another. The first was like a lion, and had eagle's wings: I beheld till the wings thereof were plucked, and it was lifted up from the earth, and made stand upon the feet as a man, and a man's heart was given to it. And behold another beast, a second, like to a bear, and it raised up itself on one side, and it had three ribs in the mouth of it between the teeth of it: and they said thus unto it, Arise, devour much flesh After this I beheld, and lo another, like a leopard, which had upon the back of it four wings of a fowl; the beast had also four heads; and dominion was given to it. After this I saw in the night visions, and behold a fourth beast, dreadful and terrible, and strong exceedingly; and it had great iron teeth: it devoured and brake in pieces, and stamped the residue with the feet of it: and it was diverse from all the beasts that were before it; and it had ten horns (Daniel 7:2-7).

It is striking that the first three empires are easily identifiable — a lion, a bear, and a leopard — but the fourth beast can neither be named nor can it be described as having the characteristics of any existing animal. It is completely diverse. This is doubtless the foundation of democracy; the people of the world are in charge of their own destiny.

What's Wrong with Democracy?

There is nothing wrong with democracy on the surface; after all, this system guarantees more freedom, justice, and happiness for the individual than any other. But the deception begins when the belief turns into fanaticism to the point that one is convinced the world will live in peace and harmony under democracy. Therefore, when we view democracy in a critical light, we need not search for hidden evils that will emerge or that will usher in the reign of the Antichrist, but rather the normal daily activities of eating and drinking, marrying and giving in marriage, buying and selling, and planting and building.

The Time of Noah

Let's consider the account contained in Luke 17:26-27: "And as it was in the days of Noe, so shall it be also in the days of the Son of man. They did eat, they drank, they married wives, they were given in marriage, until the day that Noe entered into the ark, and the flood came, and destroyed them all." No particular sin is mentioned here, only normal daily activities — we still eat and drink, marry and give into marriage. Human behavior has not changed since the days of Noah.

Obviously believers also eat, drink, marry and are given in marriage but there is a difference: while we go about these daily tasks in life, we are simultaneously preparing for the return of our Lord: "Looking for that blessed hope, and the glorious appearing of the great God and our Saviour Jesus Christ" (Titus 2:13).

Lot and Sodom

Jesus also compared His Second Coming with the time of Lot: "Likewise also as it was in the days of Lot; they did eat, they drank, they bought, they sold, they planted, they builded; But the same day that Lot went out of Sodom it rained fire and brimstone from heaven, and destroyed them all. Even thus shall it be in the day when the Son of man is revealed" (Luke 17:28-30).

Again, the Lord lists the normal daily activities of people, and again He emphasizes, "Thus shall it be in the day when the Son of man is revealed." The Lord used the examples of Noah and Lot's time as signs of the terrible day that is yet to come: the Great Tribulation. Therefore, it is wrong to look for some hidden political agenda or conspiracy by the world bankers, political leaders, or some obscure organization. Rather, we are instructed to look at the normal daily activities in which people place their hope on a better world, more righteousness, peace, and prosperity, without the Prince of Peace, the Lord Jesus Christ.

To identify this final kingdom in prophecy, we are required to analyze a new political system and pinpoint a philosophy that is incomparable with any others in the history of mankind. Such a system and philosophy is being developed in Europe today.

Europe Today

Not only is the European Union uniting geographically through economics and politics, but the unthinkable is also taking place today: the Union is also uniting religiously. The most diverse continent in the world is unifying! Furthermore, Europe is looking to the East to prepare former communist countries for integration into the European Union! The Romans would have caused the union by force. Now it is being accomplished peacefully through democracy.

The following report was published in the April 2, 1994 edition of *The Daily Mail*:

> Hungary was the FIRST FORMER COMMUNIST BLOC COUNTRY to apply to join the European Union, saying it needed membership to "GUARANTEE SECURITY AND INTEGRITY." Hungary's bid to move into the western economic system is likely to be followed this month by Poland and later by the Czech Republic.[19]

Notice that the year in which this was published is 1994. The original copy for the text of this book was written during that time. Things have changed dramatically since then. I did a search on the Europa website and found the following information under the heading "Enlargement":

> From six members in the 1950s to 25 in 2004 and 27 in 2007. The European Union can now rightly claim to represent a continent. Scratching from the Atlantic to the Black Sea, it reunites Europe's eastern and western parts for the first time since they were split by the Cold War 60 years ago.

It is clear from this article that political realities will change but prophecy does not. The European Union is the avenue by which the world will become one. This is an excellent example of democracy moving to the East instead of communism moving West, as has been feared for decades. Social/capital democracy is the only remaining alternative since the fall of communism.

We are hard hit when we realize that democracy is the key to the New World Order that opens the door for Satan to install the Antichrist as its head. We have been taught that liberty can only come when men can choose leaders under a system of democracy, but that's wishful thinking and is also contrary to prophetic Scripture.

Praises for Democracy

Quite often I have heard believers in churches pray and praise God for the free government of democracy. I also choose democracy! I am not someone who has been taught that democracy is the best system of government, but one who personally experienced a great deal of suffering through national socialism and communism. I know what it means because I was there!

I would be guilty before God, however, if I ignored the biblical reality that when men rule themselves, which has increasingly become the case, the result will lead to the greatest catastrophe the world has ever known.

Three Endtime Proofs

Someone may now ask: "Are you sure the Bible speaks about democracy as being the last Gentile government?" Yes, I am absolutely sure, because it is the last world empire. How do I know it's the last one? Here are three main reasons:

1) The Jews are returning to the land of Israel: "And I will bring them out from the people, and gather them from the countries, and will bring them to their own land, and feed them upon the mountains of Israel by the rivers, and in all the inhabited places of the country" (Ezekiel 34:13).

2) The land has been resurrected from the dead: "But ye, O mountains of Israel, ye shall shoot forth your branches, and yield your fruit to my people of Israel; for they are at hand to come" (Ezekiel 36:8).

3) Jerusalem is a Jewish city after 2,500 years: "And in that day will I make Jerusalem a burdensome stone for all people: all that burden themselves with it shall be cut in pieces, though all the people of the earth be gathered together against it" (Zechariah 12:3).

God's Word says that these events will take place before the Great Tribulation, the final seven years during which the New World Order, led by the Roman European model, will exist as the final empire. Fulfillment of prophecy is proof that we live in the last times and therefore the system of government that prevails during those times must be the last one.

The Clay

We have established that the last world empire consists of a mixture of iron and clay. We revealed that iron symbolizes the ancient Roman power structure and the clay represents the power of the people, the idea embodied in the practice of democracy.

You will find a large number of prosperous Jews in areas where democracy has been practiced for generations. Therefore, I submit that the clay represents the Jewish people and their attempt to integrate into the New World Order. The Bible provides a clear answer as to who the clay represents: "But now, O LORD, thou art our father; we are the clay, and thou our potter; and we all are the work of thy hand" (Isaiah 64:8). No other group of people has been integrated into the world to the same extent as the Jews and yet retained their identity! Frederick the Great of Prussia once asked his advisor to provide him with proof of God's existence. The advisor replied, "The Jews your majesty, the Jews!" One does not need to do much research to see that the Jews have been at the center of success in virtually all nations! The Jews had no political power until Israel was founded in 1948. The Jews always were subject to other nations but this changed dramatically with the founding of the state of Israel. Israel has become a nation and the Jews have stood their ground against an overwhelming majority of enemies.

Israel has literally been resurrected from an unproductive desert land to an agricultural powerhouse. The Jews have built a military force from the ground up. Actually, no other air force can match the skill of Israel's fighter pilots. Although brand new, Israel is no longer considered a developing country, and generously gives foreign aid to many countries.

Israel's Gross National Product per capita will exceed that of the United States in just a few years. Israel is a modern-day miracle! The country is quickly moving into high-tech, which is a good sign for the future. More and more nations today are establishing diplomatic and economic relations with Israel.

The Covenant of Rome with Israel

Reuter's news service wrote about Israel's covenant with the Vatican in a story filed on December 29, 1993:

> In a landmark step after 2,000 years of strained Christian-Jewish relations, Vatican and Israeli negotiators approved a document in which the Holy See and the Jewish state formally recognize one another. The document, the most important step in Israeli-Vatican relations since the Jewish state was founded in 1948, was given final approval by delegations which had worked on the accord for 17 months.
>
> Vatican spokesman Joaquin Navarro-Valls said the accord may make it easier for the Vatican to play a greater role in con-

> structing Middle East peace. In the preamble, the Vatican and Israel agree on the singular significance of the Holy Land.[20]

Israel became intoxicated with joy when relations between the Vatican and Jerusalem were established. Shimon Peres made the following statement:

> This is an historic act. This is not only an agreement on the establishment of relations between the Vatican and the State of Israel, but it is also a change in the long, twisting, painful pattern of relations between two great religions — the Christian and the Jewish...I hope a day will come when a third partner will join this agreement: the Muslim partner.[21]

Peace is the Prize

The Jews are willing to compromise in order to have peace in the land of Israel. At this stage, peace can only be achieved through negotiations, which means that large portions of the Promised Land and sovereignty over Jerusalem must be relinquished to their enemies. The result of these negotiations will mean peace for Israel and the Arab world and the explosion of the Middle East into a new powerhouse!

The Four World Empires Alive Today

Remnants of the four world empires still exist today as identifiable entities. Even more significant is the fact that in recent decades all four have been involved in military conflicts. For example, today's

Iraq occupies the area of ancient Babylon [the gold empire]. Persia [the silver empire] is modern-day Iran. These two nations were involved in a war that lasted from 1980-1988. Greece [the bronze empire] warred against Turkey in 1974 over the island of Cyprus. Even today, there is still an ongoing tension between them. Rome [the iron empire] was heavily involved during the Gulf conflict against Iraq in 1991. Rome, identified in the Bible as Mystery Babylon, opposed the old Babylon [Iraq] in this war.

Rome Attacking Iraq?

What evidence is there to substantiate my statement that Rome was the force that went against Iraq? There are a number of valid reasons:

1) The United States, which supplied major military force, operated under the auspice of the United Nations. We must remember that 87 percent of U.S. citizens descend from European immigrants who by culture are Romans.

2) Europe [Rome] and Japan paid for the war against Iraq. American soldiers literally became Roman mercenaries.

I realize that this may come as a shock, but according to international law, it is a correct statment. If a soldier fights for the interest of another country and gets paid by another nation then he is considered a mercenary. Europe (Rome) paid American soldiers to fight for the interest of a third party, which in this case was the nation of Kuwait.

For the first time in modern history, we saw virtually all nations unite against one nation, Babylon [Iraq]. Let's not overlook this important fact. While it was an overt victory for the allied coalition over Iraq, the war ended too soon for Israel.

The Kansas City Star carried this report on January 15th, 1995:

> **Bush Shocked Shamir**
>
> Former Israeli Prime Minister Yitzhak Shamir said he and his cabinet ministers "almost fell off our chairs" when President Bush decided to end the 1991 Persian Gulf War before Iraqi leader Saddam Hussein was toppled. His air force commander described secret Israeli reconnaissance flights over Iraq, clandestine contacts with Jordan's King Hussein and tough bargaining with the Americans, who wanted to keep Israel out of the fighting at any price.[22]

Israel's intention was to eliminate Iraq's military threat but it did not happen. Once again, foreign powers dictated Israel's course of action!

As we have just seen, remnants of all four Gentile world empires exist today. They must be identifiable; otherwise, Daniel 2 cannot be fulfilled, for it specifically states that all four world empires, including the fifth one of iron and clay, will be destroyed by the Stone, which is the Lord Jesus Christ. It stands to reason that you can't destroy something that does not exist.

Mystery Babylon in Jesus' Time

The prophetic Word reveals that the same people that destroyed Jerusalem and the Jewish temple will be in charge again when those things are restored. Let's read Daniel 9:26-27:

> And after threescore and two weeks shall Messiah be cut off, but not for himself: and the people of the prince that shall come shall destroy the city and the sanctuary; and the end thereof shall be with a flood, and unto the end of the war desolations are determined. And he shall confirm the covenant with many for one week: and in the midst of the week he shall cause the sacrifice and the oblation to cease, and for the overspreading of abominations he shall make it desolate, even until the consummation, and that determined shall be poured upon the desolate.

Verse 26 describes history. The temple in Jerusalem was destroyed by "the people of the prince that shall come." The Romans were the "people" who destroyed the temple and Jerusalem in 70 A.D. The "prince" refers to the Antichrist who will come from the revived Roman Empire. It tells of a certain covenant that will be confirmed by the "prince" for one week of years (seven years). The "overspreading of abomination that makes desolate" has not yet taken place, but it will during the Great Tribulation.

The Lord Jesus emphasized this fact in Matthew 24:15: "When ye therefore shall see the abomination of desolation, spoken of by Daniel the prophet, stand in the holy place." Thus, the same people must rule when Christ returns. Rome ruled when Jesus came to earth the first time, and Rome must rule when Jesus returns. Again, it seems necessary to emphasize that when we speak of Rome, we mean Europe, which has dominated every facet of civilization for the past 2,000 years. Therefore, I venture to say that Israel and the former Roman Mediterranean countries will be accepted into the European Union in the future. When this acceptance takes place, Europe (Rome) will dominate world finances, trade, military, religion, and world energy sources!

Mystery Babylon Not Found in Iraq

We have already established Mystery Babylon's identity in Chapters 7 and 8, but we must reiterate that information because in recent years a number of people have attempted to identify New York City as Mystery Babylon. Others have speculated that Saddam Hussein was rebuilding some of the ruins of the original Babylon and that this would be Mystery Babylon when it was completed. It was proposed that the city will be reconstructed and become the most significant city, enabling it to establish world authority.

According to my understanding of Scripture only Rome meets the biblical description of Mystery Babylon.

Let us re-read Revelation 18:3: "For all nations have drunk of the wine of the wrath of her fornication, and the kings of the earth have committed fornication with her, and the merchants of the earth are waxed rich through the abundance of her delicacies."

Here is a unique identification: the kings of the earth are the political leaders and the merchants of the earth represent the economic and financial institution of the world. The mixture between politics and religion is clear. The key word is fornication. The Greek word for fornication suggests harlotry, unlawful lust, or idolatry. Here's the connection: the Apostle Paul testified: "To all that be in Rome, beloved of God, called to be saints: Grace to you and peace from God our Father, and the Lord Jesus Christ. First, I thank my God through Jesus Christ for you all, that your faith is spoken of throughout the whole world" (Romans 1:7-8). But in 324 A.D., the Church became integrated into Emperor Constantine's political/economic system, thus, the Church has committed "fornication" with the kings and merchants of the earth! The Church of Jesus Christ has been given no political mandate in the Word of God; therefore, we have absolute assurance that since the Vatican is recognized by the entire world as a political identity, then Rome is characterized in Revelation 18:3 as the one committing fornication with the kings of the earth!

Meanwhile, how the Vatican is reaching for world religious leadership can be seen from the following newspaper report:

> Pope John Paul II spoke with warmth of his friendship for the Jewish community and his respect for the Jewish faith, his recognition of the right of Israel to exist, and the disturbing memories from his youth in occupied Poland of the Holocaust...His "greatest dream," he is telling friends and visitors these days, is to go there (Jerusalem) on a religious pilgrimage as soon as possible.
>
> He had visited the Holy Land as a bishop more than 20 years ago, but a return to Jerusalem as pope has a crucial spiritual and peacemaking meaning for him. Israel has already invited him for a state visit.
>
> "We trust," the pope said, "that with the approach of the year 2000, Jerusalem will become the city of peace for the entire world and that all the people will be able to meet there, in particular the believers in the religions that find their birthright in the faith of Abraham."[23]

While the pope's statement incorporates ecumenical religious overtones, one cannot avoid detecting the political aim by his emphasis that "Jerusalem will become the city of peace for the entire world."

We would make a great error by underestimating the deep desire of the pope, the Vatican, the European Union, and Israel for unity and peace to be achieved at any cost.

CHAPTER 10

HOW EUROPE WILL LEAD THE WORLD

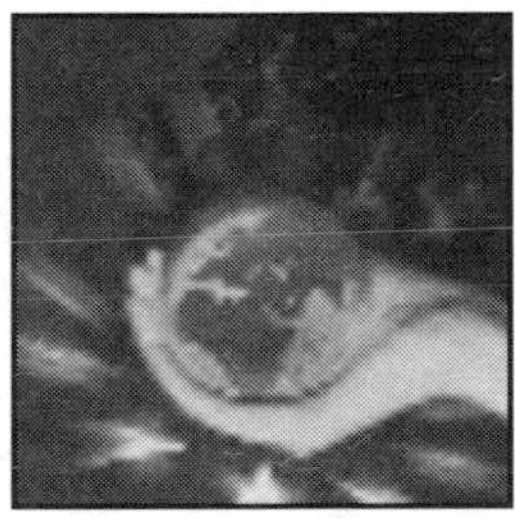

Contrary to all other nations which have been established on the motto, "United We Stand, Divided We Fall," Europe's motto is "United in Diversity." We are immediately reminded of Daniel 7:7: "After this I saw in the night visions, and behold a fourth beast, dreadful and terrible, and strong exceedingly; and it had great iron teeth: it devoured and brake in pieces, and stamped the residue with the feet of it: and it was diverse from all the beasts that were before it; and it had ten horns." Thus, it becomes clear that unity can only be achieved through diversity. After all, Muslims don't want to be Christians and Hindus and Buddhists aren't looking to change religions either. The same line of thinking is true for nationalities, thus, unity in diversity opens the door for all people to be unified under one umbrella.

How Europe Will Lead the World

Let's unpack the phrase, "These have one mind." Even today we are witnessing the uniting of the nations, which will ultimately lead to the fulfillment of prophecy as described in the above verse. Europeans are the most unity-seeking people in the world.

America: A Picture of Unity

Europe has looked enviously at America for the last 100 years. Americans had bigger houses, better cars, more luxuries, and the land was at peace: the dream of uniting.

Although the population of the United States was made up predominantly of Europeans, they were doing much better than their cousins in Europe. Why? The answer can be found in the old adage, "United we stand, divided we fall."

The United "States" Never Really Became States

The original idea for the role of state and federal government never materialized. The states never became sovereign; otherwise, America would have experienced similar problems as Europe.

Each state would have become an independent, sovereign nation with its own currency, laws, borders, and military force. One could only imagine that independent states would select the language and culture of the majority of the ethnic groups that settled there.

A duplicate of Europe would have been realized.

America was on its way to becoming a series of independent states, but the idea was crushed by the Civil War, which finally resulted in the solidification of the nation as one. Instead of becoming states in the truest sense of the word, the United States became a group of provinces of Washington D.C.

Peace Through Unity Not War

Instead of uniting, Europe became more divided than ever during the time of America's success. Two world wars were fought, which did not help to unite the people. Communism divided eastern and western Europe after World War II, but these events changed the European consciousness. It was understood that peace and prosperity could not be established by using military force.

The Awakened European Spirit of Unity

The Treaty of Rome was signed in 1957. This was the first step toward a new unity. Proposals were made at the beginning to cooperate on the level of trade and commerce, and no indication was made at that time for further unity in any other way. Today, the European Union has become a force with which to be reckoned.

Now let's read Revelation 17:13-14, which contains a description of the leadership of the last Gentile power structure: "These have one mind, and shall give their power and strength unto the beast. These shall make war with the Lamb." Unity, a characteristic not historically attributed to Europe, will be required in order to wage war against the Lamb. It is important to point out that this Scripture does not exclusively refer to a geographic area or a political identity, but more so of a demonic entity, which is revealed in the phrase, "to wage war against the Lamb." No earthly identity has the capacity to wage war against a heavenly identity.

It is important to keep in mind when reading the prophetic Word that the nations directly opposing the God of heaven are demonic forces that incite the nations to do evil against the Lord God of creation. For that reason, the Bible refers to the devil as the god of this world.

I will go into further detail later regarding the progressive development of the European Union, but for now, I want to emphasize its dynamic power. *The State* newspaper printed the following story on December 12, 1994:

> Leaders of the 12 [now 15, for the meantime] European Union nations agreed to begin open — ended discussions about membership for six Eastern European countries without setting a timetable for any of them to join.
>
> Top officials from all six European countries that now have association agreements with the European Union — Poland, the Czech Republic, Slovakia, Romania, Bulgaria and Hungary

> — met with the leaders at the Villa Hugel. The European Union said they hoped to include the six countries plus the three Baltic republics and Slovenia in a series of studies and regular meetings on how to prepare them for membership in the world's largest trading and political cooperation group.[24]

This, of course, is old news, but today we recognize that the spirit of unity in Europe has become a reality.

Why Europe Must Lead the World

Virtually all European nations will agree that their greatest glory was established during the Roman Empire. That empire is doubtlessly the center stage, not only of European history, but for literally the entire world. Rome and Europe must be credited as the founders of the world's westernized civilization, as well as the birth of democracy. Today, democracy is the indisputable world ideology in virtually all political systems, but Europe is the major influence on Western civilization.

1) It is the center of the world geographically.

2) It is the center of philosophy that has shaped the progressive civilization of the world.

3) It is the center of trade, commerce and finance.

4) It is the center and leader of religion in the world. There is no individual on earth more powerful in religion that directly affects politics than the pope of Rome.

For example, many South and Central American

nations will not allow the election of a president who is not Roman Catholic. These cultures have been inundated by Vatican philosophy.

It is important to emphasize that Rome is not limited to Europe but it is worldwide! When the pope travels the world, he draws crowds that could easily dwarf any other individual, including top political leaders. People hang on to his every word. He is considered infallible, and his church teaches that he is the only representative of Christ on earth. Crowds bow at his feet and individuals are considered privileged to kiss his ring. They long to be touched and blessed by this white-robed icon.

Europe Imitates Israel

I would like to point out here that these four characteristics were actually meant for Israel.

1) Israel is the center of the earth: "Thus saith the Lord GOD; This is Jerusalem: I have set it in the midst of the nations and countries that are round about her" (Ezekiel 5:5). Martin Luther translated Ezekiel 38:12 as, "Dwelling in the midst of the earth." And the Hebrew Tanakh says, "Living at the center of the earth."

2) Israel is the center of wisdom: No one can compare with the wisdom of King Solomon: "And all the earth sought to Solomon, to hear his wisdom, which God had put in his heart" (1 Kings 10:24).

3) Israel is to be the center of commerce and

finance: "For the Lord thy God blesseth thee, [Israel] as he promised thee: and thou shalt lend unto many nations, but thou shalt not borrow; and thou shalt reign over many nations, but they shall not reign over thee" (Deuteronomy 15:6).

4) Israel is the center of true religion: "And there was given him dominion, and glory, and a kingdom, that all people, nations, and languages, should serve him: his dominion is an everlasting dominion, which shall not pass away, and his kingdom that which shall not be destroyed" (Daniel 7:14). This verse refers to the reign of the Messiah in Israel, not the "prince," which will come from the revived Roman Empire.

Europe Wants to Replace Israel

The prophetic shadow being cast today reveals that Europe is attempting to imitate Israel; therefore, it is not surprising that the European flag contains 12 stars in a circle, not 27, or whatever the final number of Union member nations may become. Europe's constitution requires that only 12 stars should represent all nations that join the Union. We don't need much of an imagination to see that the 12 stars imitate Israel in two ways: 1) the 12 tribes of Israel and 2) the 12 apostles of the Lamb! As already mentioned, the spirit of Europe is not geographically limited to Europe. Let me explain.

The West

Over 500 years ago, a Roman Catholic Jew named Christopher Columbus discovered America. Spain claimed the entire continent in the name of the Roman church. The United States, Canada, and the nations of South America are made up primarily of European descendants. Our governments are based on Roman principles. The supreme council of ancient Rome was called the Senate. This identical system is used today in the United States, Canada, Italy, France, Ireland, South Africa, and Australia, just to name a few. So our history ties us to the Roman Empire. And even though there has been a time of apparent separation, the four corners of the world will return to its roots under the revived Roman Empire.

The East

Australia also has its roots in the European civilization. Ninety-two percent of its population is of European descent. If we analyzed the governments of Japan, Korea, Hong Kong, India, Taiwan, and other progressive Asian countries, we would find that they, too, are based on the principles of western European civilization.

The infrastructure of virtually all nations — government, education, transportation, communication, business transactions, laws, etc. — are based on the European way of doing things.

India, the world's largest democracy, is a British creation. Although the country has tried for many decades to implement Hindi as its national language, English remains the language of communication in India. Indians, whose mother tongue is not Hindi, but one of 1,652 dialects, refuse to accept Hindi as India's national language; subsequently, they must communicate with one another in English!

The South

Africa lies to the south of Rome. Fifty percent of the continent speaks French. Forty percent speak English (Africa is modeled after European laws and culture; therefore, Africa also falls under the jurisdiction of the spirit of Rome. Southern European countries view Africa as a neglected continent. European Union members would like to see such African nations brought into the fold. Mediterranean nations have long complained that the European Union is facing the wrong way. They claim that while it focuses its attention on Eastern Europe, a much greater threat looms from the south. They claim that Islamic fundamentalists will seize power in the North African countries and unleash a wave of emigration if they don't act. The following quote was written in the March 9, 1995 issue of *The European*:

> Will the southern governments succeed in persuading their northern E.U. partners to allocate more E.U. resources to

> the troubled Muslim nations of the Maghreb — Algeria, Morocco, Libya and Tunisia — across the new fault line that has replaced the Iron Curtain?
>
> Their aim is to persuade the E.U. to provide aid to develop industries in the Maghreb countries so that prosperity will reduce both emigration to Europe and support for fundamentalism.[25]

More and more Europeans are recognizing their responsibility and the danger of neglecting northern African nations. Islamic fundamentalism has become one of the world's major security risks, especially since the fall of the Soviet Union. But Muslims will not adhere to any dictate, therefore a religious compromise must be found, and can only be achieved through the Vatican. Thus, again we see Rome's influence on the world!

Religion

Europe is the center of the Gentile world. Italy is the center of Europe, Rome is the center of Italy and the Vatican is the center of Rome. The Vatican is the headquarters for the Catholic Church and for Churchianity. It appears that all major Christian denominations will ultimately become integrated under the Vatican's power structure. And Rome not only claims sole leadership of Christianity, but it will also become the leader of all other religions. How will this be accomplished? It will make accommodations for other religions outside of Christianity. This type of "umbrella" was also typical of the spirit of Rome in ancient days. The idea was, "You may worship your own god, but do so in the name of Caesar." Today the philosophy is being popularized that all people, regardless of the religion they practice, worship the one true God. They use different names for their deities, but they all have a commonality in their faiths. Here's an example:

> Pope John Paul II slipped off his shoes to sit quietly and solemnly with the supreme patriarch of Thailand's Buddhists at a Buddhist monastery in Bangkok. . . The Roman Catholic pontiff later praised the "ancient and venerable wisdom" of the Asian religion.[26]

Pope John Paul II is not the only driving force behind ecumenism, of course. Episcopalian Bishop John D. Spong wrote:

> In the fall of 1988, I worshiped God in a Buddhist temple. As the smell of incense filled the air, I knelt before three images of Buddha, feeling that the smoke could carry my prayers heavenward. It was for me a holy moment. . . beyond the creeds that each (religion) uses, there is a divine power that unites us. . . . I will not make any further attempt to convert the Buddhist, the Jew, the Hindu or the Moslem. I am content to learn from them and to walk with them side by side toward the God who lives, I believe, beyond the images that bind and blind us.[27]

Addressing a Hindu audience at the University of Calcutta, Pope John Paul II noted:

> India's mission is crucial, because of her intuition of the spiritual nature of man. Indeed, India's greatest contribution to the world can be to offer it a spiritual vision of man. And the world does well to attend willingly to this ancient wisdom and in it to find enrichment for human living.[28]

I don't believe it's necessary to belabor the point: religions will unite and Rome will lead that religious conglomeration.

Economy

Europe is pressing on towards full unity in spite of seemingly insurmountable obstacles. Geographic borders are being erased. Unity is the key word. Europe is already the economic leader of the world. We must keep in mind that this is only the beginning. It does not appear that the 15-member (27 in the meantime) nations are the complete European Union of the future. Many more nations are waiting in line to become a part of the Union. This includes many Eastern European nations. For example, Turkey is desperate to join the European Union. In an interview with *The European*, former Prime Minister Tansu Ciller said:

> It's very hard for my people to understand how countries which were in the communist bloc can move ahead of Turkey,

> which has a long association with the European Union and is a partner of NATO.[29]

America in Deep Trouble

When it became clear that Europe was emerging as an economic super state, America realized it had to make some dramatic moves to keep the pace. It was for this reason that NAFTA (North American Free Trade Agreement) was passed so quickly. In terms of trade, it joined Canada, the United States and Mexico.

Many reports during the last two decades have indicated that America is in deep trouble. One of the major problems is our government's inability to balance the budget. We have been told that the government will not even be able to pay the interest on the national debt in a few years. It is borrowing on each new annual budget. This should not surprise us, for the old Anglo-American economic system must make room for the new hybrid: European social/capitalism.

We cannot deny that our economy is becoming inferior to Europe's. And Americans are no longer dominating the financial boardrooms:

> Communism is dead and a new economic order is still to be discovered. The question of capitalism as opposed to the centrally-planned economy is that of private versus public interests and corporation versus government. We

> are at the crossroads of restructuring two conflicting forces. Three types of corporations are competing: The Anglo-American type based on share-ownership; the Japanese type, which is heavily influenced by social considerations; and the European type, which lies somewhere between the two.[30]

The Changing Times

After searching for a cheap labor nation to set up an additional assembly plant, German car manufacturer BMW chose the United States (South Carolina). The superiority of the Roman-European system was clearly demonstrated by the following fact: one manufacturing hour in Germany costs BMW $30. But in South Carolina, BMW pays only $12-$15 an hour [1994 rate]. Cheap labor is available in abundance in the United States.

U.S. Dollars for Factory Worker

	1985	**1995**
Germany	$9.60	$31.88
Switzerland	9.66	29.28
Belgium	8.97	26.88
Austria	7.58	25.38
Finland	8.16	24.78
Norway	10.37	24.38
Denmark	8.13	24.19
Netherlands	8.75	24.18
Japan	6.34	23.66

Sweden	9.66	21.36
Luxembourg	7.72	20.06
France	7.52	19.34
United States	$13.01	$17.20
Italy	7.63	16.48
Canada	10.94	16.03
Australia	8.20	14.40
Ireland	5.92	13.83
United Kingdom	6.27	13.77
Spain	4.66	12.70
Israel	4.06	10.59
New Zealand	4.47	10.11
Greece	3.66	8.95
Korea	1.23	7.40
Singapore	2.47	7.28
Taiwan	1.50	5.82
Portugal	1.53	5.35
Hong Kong	1.73	4.82
Mexico	1.59	1.51
Sri Lanka	.28	.45

(Note: The most recent figures for Luxembourg and Sri Lanka are from 1994)

This does not mean that America is going down the drain as many continue to claim. In fact, just the opposite is true. Today, the average American makes more money than ever before; we live in a better house and the cars we drive are far superior to the ones made 25 years ago. We have never had such luxury and buying power for our hourly wage. When analyzing statistics, we must consider that a new house today cannot be compared with one that was built 30 years ago.

America is not going down — it's on its way up! But Europe is rising much faster! Actually, when we consider the market potential of Africa and Asia, specifically China, we realize that the world's economic prosperity is not coming to an end, but is just beginning!

Military

As far as the military is concerned, we can summarize this way: from a political perspective, the power of military might is being transferred from the "God is Dead" power bloc (communism) to the "We are Gods" power bloc (democracy).

Furthermore, the cry for a one-world military force is being expressed more and more. An article in *The State,* dated December 3, 1993, asked:

> **EXPANSION OF NATO?**
>
> The United States proposed transforming the Cold War-era NATO alliance into a massive military and political partnership of as many as 40 nations to meet Europe's security needs. The initiative, which calls first for former Eastern adversaries of NATO to join peace-keeping operations and help draft defense budgets, was endorsed informally by foreign ministers of alliance members as "a huge step forward," Secretary General Manfred Woemer said.[31]

Fundamentally speaking, there is not much difference between NATO and the United Nations. Both have the same goal: world peace at any price.

United World Armed Forces

The United Nations is a force with which to be reckoned. There is a sensible argument that goes like this: "You can't have two armies fighting each other when there is only one." A one-world army is not a theory that exists only in the mind of some fiction writer, but it is becoming a workable reality today. The only hindrance for a world army to emerge at this moment is the United States military force. Nevertheless, Washington's financial inferiority will ultimately weaken the strong arm of the United States. When the Antichrist assumes his leadership of the world, the people will proudly ask, "Who is like unto the beast? who is able to make war with him?" (Revelation 13:4). But again, the key to world dominion will not be achieved through weapons of war, but it will be achieved through politics and economic necessity.

For example, military force did not defeat the Soviet Union, they ran out of money. One may argue that Russia, and not the U.S.A., is the hindrance to a world army. That surely was the case before the collapse of the Soviet Union, but no longer applies because Russia has an even greater financial problem than the United States. They have learned that the people will not fully cooperate with dictatorship, thus, the resurrection of a power structure equal or superior to the West is out of the question. America's desperate hold on former glory is at this moment hindering the military unity of the world. This will ultimately have to change, because the world must also become one militarily. A military superpower can only exist if it's matched by a super financial system!

How the Believer Should View these Events

How is the Church of Jesus Christ to view these developments? With joy! Nowhere in the Bible do we read that Christians have been given a political, military or geographical promise. We are pilgrims just passing through this life. The unity we see developing in the political, economic, military and religious world is just another great sign that we will be united with our Lord sooner than we may think. I believe that the words recorded in Luke 21:28 also apply to us today: "And when these things begin to come to pass, then look up, and lift up your heads; for your redemption draweth nigh."

CHAPTER 11

THE RISE OF GLOBAL UNITY

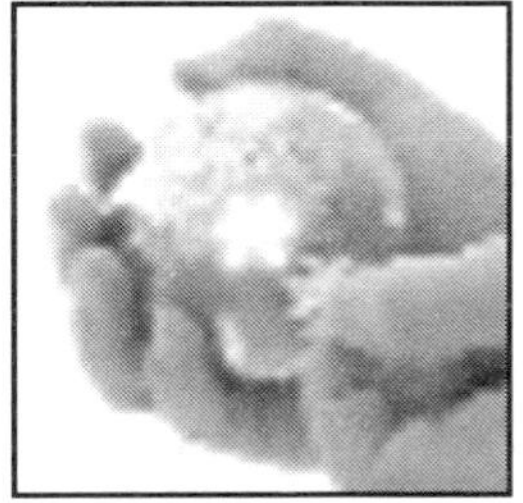

America's relationship to Rome reveals some astonishing facts: eighty-seven percent of our immigrant forefathers came from Europe. America united while Europe was divided. How Europe is changing today, and what that means to America, will be examined in this chapter. We will see how global unity is being grounded upon a new-world economy supported by the successful philosophy, "United we stand, divided we fall."

Unity of Mind

I would like to re-visit four words from Revelation 17:13: "these have one mind." This will be a great end-time miracle; namely, the near-perfect unity of people on earth after the Church has been removed. This amazing unity, however, is nothing more than Satan's imitation of the Church of Jesus Christ. Read Jesus' high priestly prayer in John 17:22-23: "And the glory which thou gavest me I have given them; that they may be one, even as we are one. I in them, and thou in me, that they may be made perfect in one; and that the world may know that thou hast sent me, and hast loved them, as thou hast loved me." In order for Satan to deceive the nations, he must produce that which looks like "they [the world] may be made perfect in one."

Unified Europe Imitates the Church

Satan's actions in the kingdom of darkness through the spirit of the Antichrist are an imitation of the Spirit of God. He is the great imitator and he will attempt to imitate the unity of the Church.

Should we then be surprised to see Rome (Europe) aim towards a goal of world dominion through a united effort? This dominance is incomparable. We live within this New World Order right now. In the past, the conqueror took possession of the territory and forced the citizens of the conquered country into submission. The same can be said about the United States. Our forefathers came to this land, conquered it, destroyed all opposition and established a new nation.

New World Order Rules

Battles for new territory are no longer fought with weapons. Now the battle takes place in political offices and corporate boardrooms as well as in the media. It is now virtually impossible to take over a country by using military force.

For example, consider Saddam Hussein's attempt to take over Kuwait. Virtually the entire world agreed to oppose Hussein's aggressive move and defeated him militarily. Why did the world oppose him? Because his action was a threat to the efforts being made towards implementing a peaceful New World Order.

Even assisting another nation without having the popular support of the people has also failed, as was the case with America's war in Vietnam. The Russians had a similar experience in Afghanistan. Shamefully defeated and embarrassed, they were forced to withdraw!

We live in a new world today where different rules and regulations apply. There won't be any need for political opinions and opposing parties once political unity has been achieved. People will believe that they have finally found a system that works to create a peaceful and prosperous society on earth. There won't be any need to keep different governments, institutions, business infrastructures, economies, commerce, industries, finance and militaries. God's Word says the people will "have one mind."

United in Diversity

Hitler did not use force to gain control of Germany,

he was democratically elected. He was able to abolish all other political parties when he saw how much support he had. The Antichrist will do likewise when he gains power and all people will become one. This follows in line with the politically correct slogan: "United in Diversity."

Someone may disagree and say that China, for example, is a communist country that is contrary to capitalist democracy. That is true, but that statement ignores the fact that China's economy is built on capitalistic principles. China is creating a gigantic export market by using the social/capital system. A modified form of communism has become a legitimate alternative in the political arena, meshing with the global democratic system that is now being built.

Four former East European countries have re-elected communists into government. More than one-third of East Germany's citizens want to go back to their communistic roots. Yes, communism is being incorporated into the idea of unity in diversity.

Global Corporations in the Lead

Multinational corporations are showing us the way. "Integrate," they say. "Let one board of directors make decisions for the smaller firms." This is a success. Larger corporations are continuously merging and buying out smaller ones. Multinational corporations have become so powerful that they are now ruling the economy, industry, finance, and even the military in the countries where they operate.

We cannot deny that the military conflict with Iraq was economically motivated. Surely we don't believe that the United States and Canada went to the Gulf to liberate the poor Kuwaitis. If we believe that, then we are likely to believe any fairy tale.

Global Corporate Identity

An article in *Focus* (a German magazine) reported that some experts had challenged the board of directors at Mercedes Benz to consider changing its standard procedure of imprinting their products with the label "Made in Germany." It was argued that many products are now being made in different countries. The proposal was to replace the "Made in Germany" label with "Made by Mercedes." Although this has not yet happened, we see the possibility of the change taking place in the near future. Most international corporations like Mercedes Benz have manufacturing or assembling facilities in dozens of countries around the world. Hence, we now see a new trend forming as multinationals expand and become more powerful.

Employees are now identified with the company they work for to such an extent that they are becoming fully integrated with the name of the company. For example, John Doe, who works for General Motors in Detroit, Michigan, would simply be identified as "John Doe of General Motors." Thus, unity based on citizenship will decrease and make room for unity through an alliance of global corporations.

20th- Century Success Story

The United States of America is perhaps the greatest success story in the last century. We have already spoken about the conflict Europe has been involved in for so many centuries. The discovery of America opened up two important avenues for the development of endtime events:

- The energy of Europeans had to be expanded, and the vast open spaces of the Americas offered the perfect opportunity for them.
- For the first time since the Roman Empire, Europeans had to work together in spite of diverse culture, language, heritage, and mentality. North America, which had a climate similar to Europe, offered the greatest opportunity.

What occurred during these short 200 years, specifically in the last 100, is now history. The experiment to have Europeans work, live, and unite under one nationality was a smashing success. Therefore, it is not surprising that many important global organizations such as the United Nations were founded in the United States. If Europeans from so many different nations, including Africa and Asia, came together and formed a successful nation, then why would this not also apply to Europe? But there is more. This system of unity created from out of diversity could also be applied to the entire world. Not only was the United

States extremely successful in industry, agriculture, politics, and religion, but the result of creating a new identity from among the diverse people of the world is even more astonishing.

Mixture of the Nation's Success

I am aware that my analysis of the United States is somewhat prejudiced. I have been an American citizen since 1967. The United States has become my country. The greatest things that can happen to anyone happened to me in the United States. God saved me in this country. He led me to my wife Ruth. My three sons were born in America. Not only are they Americans on paper as I am, but they think, act, and exhibit Americanism. In all of my travels, I have never met anyone more polite or generous as Americans.

But that's one side of the story. My love for this country should never blind me to truth, which is why I am obligated to publish the other side of the coin:

> The United States is among the least peaceful nation in the world, ranking 96th between Yemen and Iran, according to a new index released that evaluates 121 nations based on their peacefulness.
>
> "The objective of the Global Peace Index was to go beyond a crude measure of wars by systematically exploring the texture of peace," said Global Peace Index President Clyde McConaghy.

The index was compiled based on 24 indicators measuring peace inside and outside of a country. They included the number of wars a country was involved in the past five years, how many soldiers were killed overseas and how much money was made in arms sales.

Domestic indicators included the level of violent crimes, relations with neighboring countries and level of distrust in other citizens.

The results were then reviewed by a panel of international experts.

"We were trying to find out what positive qualities lead to pace," said Leo Abruzzese, the North American editorial director of the intelligence unit that is part of The Economist Group that publishes the well known magazine.

He said they found in general the most peaceful countries were the smallest, the most politically stable and democratic.

"Democracy didn't actually correlate with peace, but a well-functioning democracy did. Efficient, accountable government seems to be the leading determinant of peace. Beyond that, income helps."

Fifteen of the top 20 most peaceful nations are in Western Europe, and countries with higher income appeared to lead to higher levels of peace, he said.

The United States ranked 98th out of 121 nations, just worse than Yemen and just better than Iran, Honduras and South Africa.

Abruzzese said the United States score was pulled down by the number of wars it is involved in, large numbers of soldiers killed on the battlefield and high defense spending.

He said the fact the United States has the world's largest

prison population per share of overall population also pulled down the score.

"It also has relatively high levels of violent crime," he added.

—http://news.yahoo.com/s/nm/20070530/tx_nm/usa_peace_dc;_ylt+AmBZ

Peace and Unity

I am also convinced that numerous people from around the world have come to the same conclusion. So, why not have a one-world society?

Dear friends, this question is legitimate. It is for these and many other reasons that I have neither the time nor the energy to oppose these ideas as they are fulfillments of Bible prophecy. The world is becoming one, which means that Jesus must be coming soon; therefore, I will invest my time, energy, and finances in proclaiming the liberating Gospel of the Lord Jesus Christ to all people everywhere.

Success Story: U.S.A.

Thirty-eight million newcomers arrived in the United States between 1820 and 1940. The following is a breakdown of the major ethnic groups:

6.0 million Germans	4.7 million Italians
4.5 million Irish	4.2 million British
3.5 million Russians	2.5 million Austrians
1.5 million Swedish	

Once they arrived, they became one: one nation, one language, one currency, one government, one military, one economy, and one flag!

The United States started to prosper in the late 1800s, and was no longer considered poverty-stricken, but now Europe was in turmoil. The United States had not only become a nation to be reckoned with, but in the process, it surpassed all other nations, including Europe. In the early 1900s, the U.S. became the undisputed global leader and held the lead for about 70 years. What happened next?

The Changing of the Guard

While many of us, specifically those in the field of Bible prophecy teaching, seek an answer as to why Europe has surpassed the U.S., I propose that we look at this development as a fulfillment of Bible prophecy. How can the United States become subject to Europe if it is more powerful? How can Europe become the power center of the world if it has not surpassed all nations, including the United States?

The logical answer to these two questions is sufficient to prove beyond a shadow of a doubt that we are approaching the last stages of the endtimes, which will establish world leadership through the social/capital democratic system.

Which Land of Opportunity?

America is still a land of great opportunity, but only

for a select few: the ones who are educated and those who possess talent. We refer to an article that was published in the July 6th, 1995 edition of *The State* on page B10:

> The United States is the land of opportunity for fewer and fewer foreigners whose special skills give them the right to immigrate here, U.S. officials say.
>
> Newly released Justice Department statistics show that highly educated professionals from other countries are spurning the chance to apply for U.S. citizenship under immigration preferences for workers in key fields.
>
> In the last fiscal year, the number of immigrants legally admitted to this country for employment reasons plunged by 16 percent, mostly because eligible professionals failed to apply, officials said.
>
> Since 1993, the number of immigrant visas granted to scientists, academics, managers and others with special training declined to 123,291 from 147,012, the Justice Department reported, blaming the shortfall on a dearth of applicants.
>
> "There were fewer takers," said Greg Gagne, spokesman for the Immigration and Naturalization Service.
>
> Labor experts said the drop in applications from professionals appears to reflect a decline in the number of high-wage jobs in the U.S. economy, even as demand for low-wage workers remains high.[32]

Prophetic tendencies are revealed in the new immigration statistics. The success of the United States as a nation was due primarily to the amalgamation of nationalities. Nearly 37 million people emigrated from Europe in search of a better life. As we have seen, unity was the key; therefore, the logical question follows: If people of different nationalities can become successfully integrated into one new nation, then why can't the Europeans become united on their own continent? That is why Europe is in the process of uniting; therefore, the center of success is shifting back to Europe.

The July 1994 issue of *Money* magazine reported that 250,000 Americans were leaving the United States to search for better opportunities elsewhere. Rome (Europe) must dominate the world in order to fulfill Bible prophecy. Nations like the United States that would challenge Europe, must decrease in importance. This trend is taking place now. Europe could never challenge America on its own merits while it remained divided into individual sovereign nations. But a united Europe would be able to challenge anyone. The idea of becoming "one-minded" like the U.S. began to take root.

United Europe Under Rome

The dream of having a united Europe is not a new concept, but one that actually took place during the Roman Empire. Not one European nation can write its history without mentioning Rome. Along with its culture, glory, philosophy and politics there was a certain degree of liberation for the people who lived during the Roman era. Throughout history, philosophers and statesmen have always spoken about the unity of the Roman Empire; a power bloc that could not be challenged by any nation!

How did Rome become so powerful? The answer can be summed up with one word: unity. Rome did not enslave the people of the nations it conquered, but gave them liberty. Hollywood movies have strongly influenced our thinking in their depiction of Roman soldiers whipping people into submission. Naturally brutality did take place, but it was only resorted to as a form of punishment.

Flogging was a form of punishment in many countries — even until as recently as the mid-1900s. Britain used flogging as a form of punishment. Jews in Palestine who were caught opposing the military occupation of that land were frequently whipped!

Roman Citizenship: Europe's Desire

People who are oppressed never accomplish anything. The glorious Roman Empire was built because people wanted to become a part of this success story. They served Caesar wholeheartedly. They were proud to be called Romans. They surrendered themselves to Rome's jurisdiction and welcomed the new liberty that Caesar had guaranteed.

The Hitler Connection

The same was true during the Hitler era. People in Germany, Austria and many other countries worshiped

Adolf Hitler. They wanted this man to rule over them by whatever means necessary. They even prayed for him because they thought he was the man God had sent for salvation, peace and prosperity. Naturally, they were deceived, just as people are being deceived today by the success of democracy.

Rome conquered one nation after another, not by using only its military power, but by promising integration and offering Roman citizenship, protection and prosperity. They had a chance to become Romans. Provisions had been made for each new citizen to retain and practice his or her own culture, custom, language and religion. The plurality of gods was tolerated, but only under the name of Caesar.

"I Was Born Free"

The significance of Roman citizenship is emphasized in Scripture. Acts 22:25-29 describes an event in which Paul used his Roman citizenship to avoid being flogged:

> And as they bound him with thongs, Paul said unto the centurion that stood by, Is it lawful for you to scourge a man that is a Roman, and uncondemned? When the centurion heard that, he went and told the chief captain, saying, Take heed what thou doest: for this man is a Roman. Then the chief captain came, and said unto him, Tell me, art thou a Roman? He said, Yea. And the chief captain answered, With a great sum obtained I this freedom. And Paul said, But I was free born. Then straightway they departed from him which should have examined him: and the

> chief captain also was afraid, after he knew that he was a Roman, and because he had bound him.

Paul was a Roman who had inherited his citizenship by birth — freedom and liberty were a guarantee. This is clear from the chief captain who was a naturalized citizen and not a Roman by birth. Apparently there was a great cost involved in becoming a Roman citizen: "The chief captain answered, With a great sum obtained I this freedom." Paul simply replied, "But I was free born." In other words, he was born a Roman citizen.

U.S.A. Following in Roman Footsteps

The United States has followed in Rome's footsteps. Automatic citizenship is granted to any person who was born in the United States. The process of naturalization was developed for people who were not born in the United States but wished to become citizens — same as in Rome.

Most of us do not realize that our immigrant forefathers paid a tremendous price to become Americans. Think about those people who came to America prior to 1800 through the early 1900s. Money obviously played a big factor, but that was the least of their worries. For most people, it would be the last time they saw Europe. They went from cultured and affluent to impoverished, lawless, and sickly. Worst of all, they had to face these challenges without the support of extended family members. They relinquished their heritage, language, and national identity. Our forefathers lost virtually everything that identified them as European. Most people died in poverty and misery, but their descendants built upon their loss and experience.

A New Way for the New World

Our immigrant forefathers started something totally new without having any guarantee of success. They must have been courageous people who had faith in a new existence. Many had faith in the living God. Burning bridges to the old continent gave our forefathers a creative spirit to do things differently, which later became known as the American way!

Unlike most other colonies, which were fed intellectually, philosophically, financially and militarily by their mother country in Europe, American forefathers cut many ties, including traditional religion.

Faith in God

Faith in the living God became more important than faith in the traditional European religion. Many Americans believed the Bible was the Word of God. They preached the Gospel of salvation to whoever would listen. The result was astonishing. Hundreds of thousands of people were converted to a living faith in the Lord Jesus Christ. America became the undisputed capital of the Gospel of Jesus Christ for the entire world! Even to this day, America is responsible for most of the world's missionary activity. There's no doubt, therefore, that the success of the United States stemmed from the faith people had in the living God of the Bible.

Foreign Aid

It is not surprising that America showed compassion to its enemies. The blood of the last American soldier killed in action in Germany was not even cold when Americans started loading ships with food to feed the conquered Germans. During that time, no other nation gave as much in foreign aid as did America. It was a time when the United States was the undisputed leader in the living standards of the world.

It is striking that during the last several decades, the majority of Americans have protested against giving foreign aid. And the voices of protest are becoming louder today.

Even more astonishing is the fact that the right wing, which is overwhelmingly supported by Bible-believing Christians, now opposes foreign aid! We have to wonder if this has any relationship to the fact that America today is ranked 18th in supplying foreign aid to other countries. No less surprising is the fact that the standard of living for Americans has fallen from first place to eighth.

Religious Freedom

Freedom of religion for the sake of political union was a guarantee in the Constitution for Jews and Catholics and marked another milestone in the remarkable success story of the United States.

Even though the Catholic Church had persecuted Protestants in Europe, it was allowed to prosper here mostly unhindered, but along with religious tolerance came occultist religions.

George Washington and many of the founding fathers were members of Freemasonry. Mormonism, Jehovah's Witnesses, Christian Science, and multiple other cults are a product of religious freedom but the new nationality brought forth by the immigrants over-bridged the religious diversity.

Religion was the major hindering element for unity in Europe. Today, however, the story has changed dramatically. Religion has become insignificant throughout Europe.

Tolerance is at an all-time high because the bulk of the population does not take religion seriously but the dismal state of religious attachment has opened the door for Europeans to unite.

I would like to conclude this chapter by making an important point: we who are born again of the Spirit of God are heavenly citizens. Our home is in heaven regardless of where we live. Our position is eternally settled in heaven. We are perfectly one in the Lord Jesus Christ!

Are you born again? If not, you belong to the political identity of a nation. You have no hope, no future, and no eternal life in our Lord.

CHAPTER 12

EUROPE INTO THE FUTURE

The coming European powerhouse will produce the system that creates the ten-king empire. This chapter reviews Europe's development from 1957 to the present.

A social/capital democracy is becoming the driving force behind the Union, which will surpass all others. The New World Order is in its infant stages today, but it will soon become the established political philosophy.

Europe Into the Future

How has Europe progressed since the Treaty of Rome, which marked the beginning of the new Europe signed in 1957?

The Original Six in 1957

The following six countries were the original signatories to the Roman treaty:

Belgium 10.0 million	France 57.2 million
Germany 80.2 million	Italy 57.8 million
Luxembourg 0.4 million	Netherlands 15.1 million

Thus, a total of 220.7 million people joined in a cooperative effort to create a new Europe. Other European countries recognized the promising future associated with this new movement after the Common Market's initial success, and a number of nations applied for membership.

Three Nations Join in 1973

Three more nations were accepted in January 1973:

Denmark 5.2 million	Ireland 3.5 million
Britain 57.6 million	

Thus, another 66.3 million people were added to the Union! Now united Europe had surpassed the United States in population.

Greece Makes Ten

An eight-year lull followed 1973. Then Greece was added to the European Economic Community in 1981. This step was rather unusual. Although Greece is part of Europe, it is more identifiable in association with the Mediterranean countries and was expected to be one of the last to gain acceptance.

Greece — 10.3 Million

When Greece was added to the fold, the total population of the European Economic Community was 297 million strong. I believe there is a specific reason that Greece was added to the Union in 1981. I mentioned earlier that the Bible says that Greece was the third Gentile world empire. We also saw how the Gentile empires were listed: Babylon, Medo-Persia, Greece, and Rome, symbolized by four metals — gold, silver, brass and iron. Furthermore, we saw that these four empires are identifiable in our day and all four were involved in war in recent decades.

The enumeration of these power structures is significant: "Then was the iron, the clay, the brass the silver, and the gold, broken to pieces together" (Daniel 2:35a). Babylon, which is the head, will not be broken first, but the feet, the softest part, the most inferior system will be destroyed first. When Daniel interpreted the dream, he cautioned, "it brake in pieces the iron, the brass, the clay, the silver, and the gold" (Daniel 2:45). The iron is Rome [European

Union] and the brass is Greece. Therefore, we can expect that Iran [Persia], the silver empire, will ultimately be added as well. Finally, Iraq, which was ancient Babylon, the gold empire, must also be incorporated in the European Union power structure (Roman Empire).

While these conclusions are not clearly visible today, we know from Holy Scripture that these empires will unite because they must stand in the final judgment.

1986: Europe — 336.4 Million Strong

The European Union welcomed Portugal and Spain into the family in 1986.

Portugal 9.9 million   Spain 40.0 million

The EEC was now 336.4 million strong! Europe had become the most powerful economic bloc in the world in a little less than 30 years after the Treaty of Rome. The organization has been known as the European Union since 1994.

Who are the Ten Kings?

Many Bible scholars believe that the European Union is a fulfillment of the resurrected Roman Empire. It was also commonly believed that the European Union would consist only of ten nations, but as we have just seen, the number of members rose to 12 with the addition of Spain and Portugal. The idea that the Union would be made up of ten nations originated with the misinterpretation of Revelation 17:12, which speaks of ten kings.

A Voice from 1967

Dr. Wim Malgo, founder of Midnight Call Ministries, wrote the following in 1967: "Let us not look for ten countries being members of the European Common Market constituting the fulfillment of Revelation 17:12. Rather we must look for ten power structures that will develop through the European initiative but will be worldwide."

I have always agreed with this statement because the Bible specifically says ten kings. A king is not a nation but a person. While it is too early to properly identify what these ten power structures will be, there is no doubt that Europe will be number one. The reason is not only because Europe has a well educated population, is the biggest economic power bloc, and has other innumerable advantages, but also because Europe is the foundation of our modern civilization and is willing to change. History proves that whenever a group of people or a nation was willing to change, such as was the case with America, it reinvented itself into a new process of creative thinking.

Social/Capital Democracy

Today, America dreams of "Old Glory," while

Europe looks toward a new, unknown, but hopeful future. There is no doubt in my mind that the risk-taker will always succeed. One thing is relatively sure: none of the nations from among the presently functioning democratic system will emerge as the clear winner in Europe. Thus, compromise is the key to the success of merging the various political thinking patterns into one. Europe has strong socialist tendencies and plans to accept former communist countries as members; therefore, I believe a new system will be created that I would like to identify as a social/capital democratic system. We already mentioned that China would fiercely oppose American capitalist democracy, yet a social/capital system is acceptable.

What is Socialism?

Communism was rejected by progressive Western nations during the time of the Soviet Union. Socialism was also rejected by the United States but accepted in Europe. The United States hated the idea of socialism because it was considered a precursor to communism. But when we research the meaning of the word socialism, we quickly learn that no nation can exist without implementing its practice.

During one of our prophecy conferences, I asked the audience, "How many socialists do we have here today?" Not one hand was raised. I rephrased my question and asked, "How many of you do not have at least one insurance policy?" Two or three people raised their hands and I assume they did not quite understand my question. Then I said, "You purchase an insurance policy to protect yourself in the event that something happens to you. That's socialism!"

Do We Really Own Our Property?

One day my son, Micah, casually asked me if I had paid the lease on my house.

I answered, "I don't lease the house. I own it. I paid for it."

Then he countered, "Try not paying your lease to the local tax office and the government will take your house and lease it to someone else!"

He was right! A form of socialism can be found in all societies and cannot function without it. To be social is a form of socialism. For instance, we must be sensitive to the rules, customs and regulations of our neighborhoods. We cannot live under the false pretense that we live in a free country and can do as we please.

Let's suppose you decide not to participate in the social services available in your neighborhood. You want to be independent so you cut off your electricity, disconnect your telephone and cancel your water, sewerage, and gas accounts. Then you dig your own well for water, install your own septic tank, and start cooking on a wood-burning stove or even on an outside fire. It would not take too long before your neighbors started complaining to the authorities, and rightly so!

The accumulation of trash and the constant smoke from your fire would certainly be an unpleasant sight and smell to your neighbors, and the authorities would force you to conform to the prevailing social standard.

Socialism is also at work in America's finance and industry. Remember when the U.S. government had to bail out Chrysler Corporation from financial disaster? That, too, is socialism.

What about farmers? Here again, we see socialism in action. The government guarantees income with immense subsidies for farmers who cannot compete successfully with their products in the global market. That is not free capitalistic enterprise, it is socialism.

You won't hear any protests against socialism especially when it works! Today, not only in the United States, but in virtually all countries, with the exception of a few African nations, farmers are producing such an abundance of food that quite frequently products have to be destroyed in order to stabilize prices and avoid financial ruin. This type of socialism has always been accepted in Europe and the European's experience in that field is now helping Europe to become even more prosperous.

Europe: 15 Nations

Three more nations joined the Union on January 1, 1995.

Austria 8.0 million

Sweden 8.6 million

Finland 5.0 million

At the time of this writing, the European Union is more than 362 million strong. And many other nations, especially from Eastern Europe, are waiting to join. Therefore, it appears the European Union will continue to grow in size and number. I believe it will eventually expand across the globe and consist of ten power structures.

It is important to understand that no other group of nations but Europe can claim to be the center of the world's intellect. Our westernized civilization originated with the Europeans. No doubt, Europe is being prepared for world dominion!

United Economy

Daniel prophesied about this last kingdom approximately 2,500 years ago: "Thus he said, The fourth beast shall be the fourth kingdom upon earth, which shall be diverse from all kingdoms, and shall devour the whole earth, and shall tread it down, and break it in pieces" (Daniel 7:23). Notice Daniel wrote the last kingdom will devour "the whole earth."

At this point in time, Europe's phenomenal growth is based strictly on economy and finance. The economy is virtually united already. Europe does not have a unified currency at this time, but they are well on their way to establishing one. The following article was published on page 17 of the July 6, 1995 edition of *The European*:

Currency Target: 1999

The Cannes summit recognized that 1999 is a more realistic date than January 1, 1997, for the beginning of the final stage of monetary union, due to culminate in the changeover to a single currency. As set out by the European Commission's May, 1995 green paper, the three main steps of the final phase will be spread out over about four years.

• Late 1997: The E.U. Council decides which countries meet the convergence criteria.

• January 1998: Dates for the start of the final stage and for the introduction of the single currency are announced; the European Monetary Institute prepares to become a fully fledged central bank. Preparations for the switch to a single currency, including those for all legal contracts (such as mortgages), intensify.

• January 1999 (at the latest): Exchange rates are irrevocably fixed between participating countries; the European Central Bank (ECB) takes over; the ECU becomes a common currency in which monetary policy operations are conducted; governments issue debt in the single currency; financial markets and the private sector switch to the single currency; retail transactions are still made in national currencies.

• ..January 2002 (at the latest): All transactions in the participating countries must be denominated in the single currency. In a matter of weeks, coins and bank notes denominated in the single currency must be substituted for the "old" means of payment. Those countries not ready for monetary union must continue their efforts to meet the criteria and their currencies will remain within the exchange rate mechanism of the European monetary system.[33]

In the meantime, the euro became the official currency of 12 nations as of 1 January 2002.

Global Currency

While much doubt and uncertainty surround the Union's coming to terms with the requirements for the new currency called the euro, it doesn't take much of an imagination to see the reality of a European currency when considering how Europe looked just 50 years ago. With the coming new European currency, we will likely soon see that the price of oil will be paid in euro currency. The Organization of Petroleum Exporting Countries (OPEC) is already lamenting the continuous fall of the U.S. dollar. Many voices can be heard in favor of replacing the U.S. dollar as the world's dominant currency.

In practical terms, a world currency already exists. For example, when you use your credit card in any part of the world, you can purchase virtually anything in any currency. If you have a U.S. credit card, then you will be billed in your own currency, but the shop keeper, restaurant or hotel will be paid in their local currency. We don't have to wait for a one-world financial system to emerge because it is already at work! The world already functions as a global economic community.

Religion

This last Gentile empire will be saturated with

occultism. In fact, a devilish religion will be essential to the success of the economic system: "And in the latter time of their kingdom, when the transgressors are come to the full, a king of fierce countenance, and understanding dark sentences, shall stand up" (Daniel 8:23). Obviously, the phrase, "understanding dark sentences" reveals this king's deep involvement in the occult. Verse 24 continues, "And his power shall be mighty, but not by his own power: and he shall destroy wonderfully, and shall prosper, and practise, and shall destroy the mighty and the holy people." It is significant that his power is not his own.

The identity of this king is revealed in detail in Revelation 13. When we read the first eight verses of this chapter, we learn that this first beast, the Antichrist, possesses no power of his own, "And the dragon gave him his power, and his seat, and great authority...And they worshipped the dragon which gave power unto the beast: and they worshipped the beast, saying, Who is like unto the beast? who is able to make war with him?" (Revelation 13:2, 4). This Scripture clearly reveals that he will also be the supreme military ruler.

Then we read, "And there was given unto him a mouth speaking great things and blasphemies; and power was given unto him to continue forty and two months" (verse 5). And verse 7 reports: "And it was given unto him to make war with the saints, and to overcome them: and power was given him over all kindreds, and tongues, and nations." Thus, we repeatedly read that the Antichrist receives his power directly from Satan, the great dragon.

Antichrist and Europe

Scripture reports that the Antichrist will not have any power that has not already been given to him, which means he will probably be an insignificant person who will receive the support, prestige, and power he needs directly from Satan. Therefore, it is wrong to look for a certain personality today and label him as the coming Antichrist.

Although the Bible is not explicit about the identity of the Antichrist, it does provide the reader with some of his characteristics. For example, Daniel 8:24 reveals that he "shall destroy wonderfully." That eliminates all other systems we have had or will have at that time. Nazism failed and communism will never attain its former glory. The present form of capitalism will also be replaced with the new social/capital system that is already prospering in Europe.

Success by Deception

The success of the Antichrist and his new world system will not only be credited to his deceptive work but God will allow it. God is in absolute control. Satan may rule this world, but God is still on the throne.

Before I explain my statement, let me first quote

Amos 3:6: "shall there be evil in a city, and the LORD hath not done it?" In other words, God knows about Satan's every evil intention, and He will allow them to come to pass according to His counsel. The deception is also due to the fact that God gives people up who continuously refuse to listen to the truth, and who reject the love He has offered now for almost 2,000 years.

Thus, we read the following in 2 Thessalonians 2:11: "And for this cause God shall send them strong delusion, that they should believe a lie."

What a joy it is to read the last sentence of that verse: "but he [Antichrist] shall be broken without hand" (Daniel 8:25).

Jesus will not need to confront the evil one when He returns in great power and glory. Satan was defeated when Jesus cried out "It is finished!" while He was on Calvary's cross. But Satan's visible power will also be destroyed when Jesus returns to earth to set up His millennial kingdom: "then shall that Wicked be revealed, whom the Lord shall consume with the spirit of his mouth, and shall destroy with the brightness of his coming" (2 Thessalonians 2:8).

Focus on Europe

The success of Europe today, and its even greater success in the future, reveals that God is allowing the Roman Empire to be established.

The spirit of the Antichrist, which promotes freedom, justice, liberty, and prosperity for all people through democracy, is supported wholeheartedly by the majority of the world's population.

Today, it is virtually impossible for any nation to reject democracy. Thus, we must focus our attention on Europe and the Middle East. This is where it all began and this is where it will end. Rome ruled when Jesus was born and Rome will rule when Jesus returns!

Our Hope

Finally, I must emphasize that believers in the Lord Jesus Christ will not be integrated into this system. We are in the world, but we are not of the world. We do not place our hope in developing a better United States, a higher standard of living, or the implementation of justice and righteousness. Our home is with the Eternal One. We have not been given any promise, command or instruction to solve the political problems of this world. No matter how hard we may try we will never eliminate crime, pornography, homosexuality, corruption and abortion.

We are unable to impose justice and liberty in this world because the people of this world are not willing to bend their knee to Jesus Christ. The Bible does, however, provide these instructions: "But ye, brethren, are not in darkness, that that day should overtake you as a thief. Ye are all the children of light, and the children of the day: we are not of the night, nor of darkness. Therefore let us not sleep, as do others; but let us watch and be sober" (1 Thessalonians 5:4-6).

As believers, we must remember that God rules the entire universe, but He permits Satan, the father of lies, to do his work of deception. Thus, the people of the world today are hopeful that their own intellect will bring about peace. We know from the prophetic Word that real peace will only come when Jesus returns to establish His kingdom in Israel and rule the world with a rod of iron. The nations will become subject to the Lord. That is the only true and lasting peace that will come about. Thus, Satan is now working feverishly at bringing about a peace that is based strictly on the achievements of mankind. Democracy is one of the most successful tools Satan keeps stored in his arsenal to deceive the world.

CHAPTER 13

THE FINAL FALSE KINGDOM

In order for the last Gentile world empire to be replaced by God's kingdom, we must realize that the fake kingdom (Gentile) must be fully established. In that process, the distinction between Jews and Gentiles will be erased. The temple in Jerusalem will be rebuilt and animal sacrifices reinstituted. Then, the hidden conflict will become apparent with the Antichrist opposing Israel.

The Final False Kingdom

"And in the days of these kings shall the God of heaven set up a kingdom, which shall never be destroyed: and the kingdom shall not be left to other people, but it shall break in pieces and consume all these kingdoms, and it shall stand for ever" (Daniel 2:44).

Please note that the kingdom spoken of here, "which shall never be destroyed" is the kingdom of Israel. Although Israel was virtually nonexistent since the destruction of the temple in 70 A.D., the kingdom never ceased to exist as far as God was concerned.

God confirms the unconditional covenant He had made with David to his son Solomon. In 1 Kings 9:5 we read, "I will establish the throne of thy kingdom upon Israel for ever, as I promised to David thy father, saying, There shall not fail thee a man upon the throne of Israel." But Israel was not a visible reality for 2,000 years.

Zechariah, the father of John the Baptist, confirmed, "He [Jesus] shall reign over the house of Jacob for ever; and of his kingdom there shall be no end" (Luke 1:33). Just to make sure that this kingdom is eternal, let's read what God inspired the prophet Daniel to write: "But the saints of the most High shall take the kingdom, and possess the kingdom for ever, even for ever and ever" (Daniel 7:18).

In the last days, it will be the kingdom through

which the four Gentile empires will be destroyed: "Forasmuch as thou sawest that the stone was cut out of the mountain without hands, and that it brake in pieces the iron, the brass, the clay, the silver, and the gold; the great God hath made known to the king what shall come to pass hereafter: and the dream is certain, and the interpretation thereof sure" (Daniel 2:45). This verse describes the end of the Gentile world!

Daniel Sees Europe

I don't believe we need to further explain that all government systems will be destroyed and replaced with the kingdom of God, which will be established by the Lord Jesus Christ. We have just read the confirmation in Daniel 2:45. What is the scriptural basis for the belief that God will establish His kingdom on earth? Keep in mind that the Lord's first message was, "Repent ye: for the kingdom of heaven is at hand." Israel rejected the Messiah, thus, they rejected the kingdom, but that does not void God's eternal resolutions. The kingdom will be established!

Let's identify the time period when some of these events were fulfilled and when we can expect the final fulfillment to take place.

The Coming Prince

Daniel provides the answer in chapter 9:25-27:

> Know therefore and understand, that from the going forth of the commandment to restore and to build Jerusalem unto the Messiah the Prince shall be seven weeks, and threescore and two weeks: the street shall be built again, and the wall, even in troublous times. And after threescore and two weeks shall Messiah be cut off, but not for himself: and the people of the prince that shall come shall destroy the city and the sanctuary; and the end thereof shall be with a flood, and unto the end of the war desolations are determined. And he shall confirm the covenant with many for one week: and in the midst of the week he shall cause the sacrifice and the oblation to cease, and for the overspreading of abominations he shall make it desolate, even until the consummation, and that determined shall be poured upon the desolate.

This event took place when the Jews rebuilt the temple in Jerusalem upon returning from Babylonian captivity: "And after threescore and two weeks shall Messiah be cut off, but not for himself." Jesus Christ, the Messiah, died on the cross during the Roman occupation of Israel and Jerusalem. Thus, we know for certain that Rome ruled the world when Jesus was alive.

Who destroyed the city and the sanctuary? "And the people of the prince that shall come shall destroy the city and the sanctuary." It is a historical fact that Rome destroyed the "sanctuary," which can also be proven archaeologically. The Roman army led by Titus destroyed Jerusalem and the temple in 70 A.D.

Who is the prince referred to in the previous verse? Let's continue to read, "And the end thereof shall be with a flood, and unto the end of the war desolations are determined. And he shall confirm the covenant with many for one week: and in the midst of the week he shall cause the sacrifice and the oblation to cease, and for the overspreading of abominations he shall make it desolate, even until the consummation, and that determined shall be poured upon the desolate." So, the prince is the Antichrist, who will confirm a covenant with Israel.

We need to understand that the above verses deal with four time periods.

- The first period begins with the return of the Jewish captives to Jerusalem to rebuild the temple.
- The second period includes the renovation of the temple by King Herod under Roman jurisdiction.
- The third period begins with Rome's destruction of the temple in 70 A.D.
- The fourth period will occur during the third rebuilding of the temple. This is a future event in which animal sacrifice will be instituted.

Great Tribulation: Not Yet

Preterism is an eschatological position that teaches these things were fulfilled when the second temple was destroyed by the Romans in 70 A.D. This position is biblically incorrect. When Jesus referred to Daniel's prophecy, "when ye shall see the abomination of desolation, spoken of by Daniel the prophet," He revealed that the existence of a new temple, and the sacrificial service would be reinstituted but this has not yet taken place.

Jesus described the severity of the Great Tribulation in Matthew 24:21: "For then shall be great tribulation, such as was not since the beginning of the world to this time, no, nor ever shall be." Therefore, we know that the Great Tribulation has not yet taken place, and we cannot accept the interpretation that the Great Tribulation took place in 70 A.D. when the Romans destroyed Jerusalem and the sanctuary.

Sacrifice Reinstituted

Why will the Antichrist cause the sacrifice and the oblation to cease? One possible scenario is that representatives of religious groups and animal protection agencies might express their objections for slaughtering innocent animals, thereby putting pressure on Antichrist to put an end to the sacrifices.

Let me explain. The idea that the Antichrist will be an oppressive dictator is incorrect. He will rule the most sophisticated, civilized, well-educated democratic society in all of history.

Daniel wrote that he will come peaceably and obtain the kingdom by flatteries. The same is true today; no political candidate will be elected to office unless he is elected peaceably and presents his case with flatteries, making promises that usually are lies. The people will gladly support his policies. They will promote his economic and judicial system and will even gladly accept the Mark of the Beast. We must not overlook the fact that the entire world will worship the Antichrist, "all that dwell upon the earth shall worship him." You can only worship someone or something voluntarily.

The Antichrist will carefully monitor the people just as the president of the United States monitors the citizens and tries to please them as much as he can because he wants to be reelected. But the Antichrist wants more — he wants to be worshiped.

Animal Sacrifices Abolished

Israel will rebuild the temple and reinstitute animal sacrifices during the Great Tribulation that will hit a nerve with animal protection groups. I believe that the people will have a strong influence on the Antichrist. His decision to stop the sacrifice will take place at the zenith of his success. Not one major religious group today practices animal sacrifice as part of its worship. When the Jews implement the practice, it will certainly set them apart. No doubt, the world will support the Antichrist when he abolishes the practice.

Self-Esteem and Self-Image Worshiped

After he has appeased the animal rights activists, he

will then present himself to the people as the Savior; however, he will not become the sacrifice himself. Rather, in accordance with the world religion that will prevail at that time, which teaches that man is God, the Antichrist will proclaim that he is God. Thus, we read in 2 Thessalonians 2:4 that the Antichrist "opposeth and exalteth himself above all that is called God, or that is worshipped; so that he as God sitteth in the temple of God, shewing himself that he is God."

Now, someone may think that my idea sounds far-fetched. Surely nobody would believe someone who claimed to be God. Oh no? Take a trip to your local bookstore and you will find hundreds of titles in the religion section that clearly teaches man is God. This is not a strange concept to Eastern religions such as Hinduism. In general, the majority of the world's religions accept the theory that man has a "god nature" within himself, and in a matter of time he will progress to godhood.

Allow me to quote from Dr. Dave Breese's book, *Know the Marks of Cults* to confirm my statement that man is willing to accept a man/god:

> In 1954, Sun Myung Moon founded the "Holy Spirit Association for the Unification of World Christianity." This Korean millionaire religious promoter claims hundreds of thousands of followers worldwide and fosters in them the belief that he is the "Lord of the Second Advent," the person-

alized second coming of Jesus Christ. Moon rose out of his Presbyterian and Pentecostal background to organize a cult around a new theology that presents him as the great hope for mankind. He and his second wife are put forth as the new Adam and Eve, and their followers are the first children of a new and perfect world.

Judge Rutherford of the Jehovah's Witnesses presented himself as "God's chosen vessel" and the Watchtower organization as the final dispenser of truth.

Joseph Smith of the Mormons claimed that John the Baptist had given to him the priesthood of Aaron. As if this were not enough, he later claimed that he had received a higher priesthood, that of Melchizedek, from Peter, James, and John. His followers repeatedly claim that he has done more for the salvation of this world than any other man who has ever lived, except Jesus.

The late L. Ron Hubbard of the Scientology cult has offered himself as a higher authority than Jesus Christ or the Christian Bible. This science fiction writer has produced a devoted set of followers who have pressed millions of dollars into his hands.

.....Guru Maharaj Ji has presented himself as the "perfect master" and the "lord of the universe" and is esteemed as such by his thousands of followers across America and the world. It is ironic that this exalted personality, being a juvenile, had to get permission from a local judge to marry his 24-year-old secretary.

Meher Baba of the Bahai cult has said, "There is no doubt of my being God personified...I am the christ. ...I assert

> unequivocally that I AM infinite consciousness; I make this assertion because I AM infinite consciousness. I am everything and I am beyond everything...Before me was Zoroaster, Krishna, Rama, Buddha, Jesus, and Mohammed...My present avataric form is the last incarnation of the cycle of time, hence my manifestation will be the greatest."
>
> One of the marks of a cult is that it elevates the person and the words of a human leader to a messianic level. The predictable characteristic of a member of a cult is that he will soon be quoting his leader, whether Father Divine, Prophet Jones, Mary Baker Eddy, Judge Rutherford, Herbert Armstrong, or Buddha as a final authority. A messianic human leader has used the powers of his intelligence or personality and with them imposed his ideas and directives on the ignorant.[34]

You don't need to have too much of an imagination to see what will happen when the Church, the light of the world, has been removed from the earth. The Antichrist will have no problem deceiving the people of the world to agree that he is God and that God's chosen people, the Jews, should be eliminated.

CHAPTER 14

TRUE AND FALSE UNITY

In order for the world to unite, certain hindering elements such as political, economic, and religious diversity must first be dealt with. The drive for "Christian" unity is simultaneously derailing the Church from its mission and paving the way for the Antichrist. This chapter clearly presents what is meant by biblical unity.

True and False Unity

"Therefore wait ye upon me, saith the LORD, until the day that I rise up to the prey: for my determination is to gather the nations, that I may assemble the kingdoms, to pour upon them mine indignation, even all my fierce anger: for all the earth shall be devoured with the fire of my jealousy" (Zephaniah 3:8).

This verse identifies the reason for the gathering of the nations. It is addressed to Israel and explains that although the children of Israel will experience persecution and suffering, they should wait upon the Lord until He gathers the nations for judgment.

While we do not actually see the gathering of the nations against Israel, Zephaniah the prophet saw it 2,600 years ago. The purpose of that gathering is designed not only to oppose Israel, but it actually says "against the LORD, and against his anointed" (Psalm 2:2). Obviously these are demonic activities manifested through the nations of the world, in this case, through the leaders. Surely no one in his or her right mind would oppose the Anointed because He is not a visible manifestation on earth at this time, thus, we know that this is demonic activity. This activity will take place during Satan's bidding. Unfortunately, most people and even many Christians have accepted Satan's propaganda that our country is God's country and we are one nation under Him, but according to Scripture that is not true. When the devil tempted Satan he said, "All this power will I give thee, and the glory of them: for that is delivered unto me; and to whomsoever I will I give it" (Luke 4:6).

Someone may now object and say that God is in total control. That, of course, is correct, but God gave Satan control for a dispensation of time. Why? Because Scripture says that he who sins is of the devil, and since all have sinned, all are of the devil. This is very important because otherwise the devil will try to catch even Christians in his cunning devices by convincing someone to believe that our nation is special. That, of course, is a blasphemous insult to the Lord Jesus Christ and His work because He alone can free us from Satan's bondage.

The nations started to gather at the crucifixion of Christ, "For of a truth against thy holy child Jesus, whom thou hast anointed, both Herod, and Pontius Pilate, with the Gentiles, and the people of Israel, were gathered together" (Acts 4:27). This Scripture reveals the deeper truth of the crucifixion and its participants: King Herod, Pilate, the Gentiles and Israel. There you have a representation of the entire world gathering against the Anointed — a half-Jew, a Roman, the Gentiles and the Jews!

Salvation or Judgment?

God will gather the nations and pour out His fierce anger upon the earth. The purpose is two-fold: for the salvation of Israel and for the judgment of the world.

A similar event, although on a smaller scale, happened many thousands of years ago when Israel was liberated from slavery in Egypt. There was also a two-fold purpose for that event: the judgment and destruction of Egypt and the salvation of Israel.

God's Resolutions Never Change

We must never think that God has disassociated Himself from the Jewish people, the world, or His Church. He allows men to exercise his free will. God is love and love comes only on a free-will basis but this fact does not interfere with the daily developments in our world. God's eternal resolutions will never change regardless of how Israel, the Church of Jesus Christ, or the nations behave toward Him.

The Love of God

We should never think that our prayers have the power to change God's will. God will changes us through prayer. When we pray, we enter the presence of the Holy God and in so doing we will realize as did the prophets that we are nothing but dust. Thus, we will tremble and weep before the countenance of our Creator. We will experience change, even though the world around us may not change. We will also recognize the good news: God still loves His creation in spite of our rebellion, disobedience and arrogant behavior against Him.

John 3:16 is a powerful summation of the entire Bible: "For God so loved the world, that he gave his only begotten Son, that whosoever believeth in him should not perish, but have everlasting life." Because God is love, He chooses to give. He offers eternal life based on this love. Salvation cannot be earned by good deeds; it is a free gift. Despite receiving this amazing gift, we often neglect to spend time in communion with God; thus, we grow cold and lose sight of the fact that God really does love us.

God's love is incomparable to anything in this world. Our Lord is long-suffering. He is not bound by time. But when the time comes for Him to carry out His resolutions, He will command the fulfillment of His prophecies.

Work Until the Trumpet Sounds

When the trumpet sounds, it will be too late for anyone to join His Church if they are not already a believer at that time: "For the Lord himself shall descend from heaven with a shout, with the voice of the archangel, and with the trump of God: and the dead in Christ shall rise first: Then we which are alive and remain shall be caught up together with them in the clouds, to meet the Lord in the air: and so shall we ever be with the Lord" (1 Thessalonians 4:16-17). Therefore, it is our holy duty to proclaim the Gospel to all men everywhere and by all means possible as long as there is still time to do so! And according to what we see as far as Bible prophecy fulfillment is concerned, there isn't much time left!

If we are believers in Jesus Christ, then we are obligated to further the name of Christ with our prayers and financial support. We must work while it is yet day, for the night is coming when no man can work.

The Good and Bad of Evil

The progression of evil can have a mixed effect. That is one reason we must understand why the world is becoming one.

Let us look at the promise God made to Abraham: "And he said unto Abram, Know of a surety that thy seed shall be a stranger in a land that is not theirs, and shall serve them; and they shall afflict them four hundred years." Verse 16 contains the specific reason for the 400-year captivity: "But in the fourth generation they shall come hither again: for the iniquity of the Amorites is not yet full" (Genesis 15:13). This is an amazing prophecy because Israel didn't even exist during the time it was spoken. The promise was addressed to Abraham who had no children.

Why Slavery for 400 Years?

Why did God lead Israel into slavery for 400 years? Why didn't God kick the Amorites out of the land right away? We already mentioned that God is love; He had to give the Amorites another chance, an amazing 400 years, until they filled the measure of evil and sin against God.

Remember, Christ died for us while we were yet

sinners! Israel had to learn obedience during those 400 years. You can't obey God if you have not learned to obey man. In Scripture, children are admonished to obey their parents and parents are instructed to obey the government (Romans 13).

Israel experienced firsthand how evil men can be. The children of Israel were made slaves to the Egyptians and the Egyptians, in turn, murdered their newborn sons. That was a lesson that would never be forgotten!

Sodom and Gomorrah

Another example of evil's progression is found in the story of Sodom and Gomorrah. These two cities were so filled with evil that they were marked out for destruction. Righteous Lot however was the hindering element to God's destruction of those places. So what did God do? In Genesis 19:22 we read that God sent an angel to Lot with an urgent message: "Haste thee, escape thither; for I cannot do any thing till thou be come thither. Therefore the name of the city was called Zoar."

I am overwhelmed by this example of God's faithfulness and love for Lot. The execution of His judgment was hindered by Lot's action: "I cannot do any thing until thou be come thither." God's hands were bound to Lot's decision.

Righteous Lot

Lot's indecision is an obvious factor in this

account. Although he is called righteous, his testimony to his family was not very effective: "And Lot went out, and spake unto his sons in law, which married his daughters, and said, Up, get you out of this place; for the LORD will destroy this city. But he seemed as one that mocked unto his sons in law" (Genesis 19:14). His own sons-in-law did not take his warning seriously.

Lot remained undecided until the last minute. We read in the next verse: "And when the morning arose, then the angels hastened Lot, saying, Arise, take thy wife, and thy two daughters, which are here; lest thou be consumed in the iniquity of the city" (verse 15).

The angels even had to use physical force to get Lot to comply: "And while he lingered, the men laid hold upon his hand, and upon the hand of his wife, and upon the hand of his two daughters; the LORD being merciful unto him: and they brought him forth, and set him without the city" (verse 16).

When will judgment come upon the world? When the righteous have been removed from the earth! That is another urgent reason we should prepare ourselves for the Rapture of the Church!

The Church Hinders the Antichrist

In the New Testament, we read about a hindering element for the progression of evil: the revelation of the Antichrist. In 2 Thessalonians 2:6-7 we read, "And now ye know what withholdeth that he might be revealed in his time. For the mystery of iniquity doth already work: only he who now letteth will let, until he be taken out of the way."

Only after the Church has been removed from this earth can the Antichrist be revealed: "And then shall that Wicked be revealed, whom the Lord shall consume with the spirit of his mouth, and shall destroy with the brightness of his coming" (verse 8).

The Antichrist embodies the power of darkness and therefore he cannot be revealed in his full capacity of evil while there is still light. Nor can the full power of the wicked one develop until the people are united behind him. Revelation 13:8 reads, "And all that dwell upon the earth shall worship him." This unity will not come about instantaneously, but the preparation for it is in full swing today.

This prophecy cannot be fulfilled while the Church is on earth — she must be raptured!

The Perfect Unity of the Church

The ecumenical movement, the World Council of Churches, and various movements and organizations that try to unify Christianity are actually working against the will of God because the Church, the body of believers, is already perfectly united in the Lord Jesus Christ.

We may attend different denominational or non-denominational churches, or be members of other groups that come together to hear the Word of God and break bread, but we are already perfectly united in the Lord Jesus Christ!

The Fulfilled Unity of the Church

If we are already perfectly one, then how do we explain John 17:23: "I in them, and thou in me that they may be made perfect in one." This verse seems to imply that Jesus wants the churches to unite. To understand this passage properly, we must read verse 20: "Neither pray I for these alone, but for them also which shall believe on me through their word." Here it is revealed that Jesus is prophesying that others will believe in Him through the preaching of His disciples. In John 17, He refers four times to the idea that they may be one!

Gentiles Added to the Church

When the Church of Jesus Christ was born on Pentecost, all of its members were Jews, and the Gentiles were added later. Many Jews who believed in Jesus also believed that the Gentiles had to become Jews first. In other words, they had to keep the law in order to be saved: "But there rose up certain of the sect of the Pharisees which believed, saying, That it was needful to circumcise them, and to command them to keep the law of Moses" (Acts 15:5). The Apostle Paul, however, makes it clear that their belief was wrong: "And God, which knoweth the hearts, bare them witness, giving them the Holy Ghost, even as he did unto us; And put no difference between us and them, purifying their hearts by faith" (Acts 15:8-9). Thus, Gentile believers became one with Jewish believers.

This perfect unity is later demonstrated by the Apostle Paul, when he wrote the following in Galatians 3:28: "There is neither Jew nor Greek, there is neither bond nor free, there is neither male nor female: for ye are all one in Christ Jesus." This unity is not something that will be achieved in the future; it is a reality right now, just as it was almost 2,000 years ago.

Spiritual Unity

It is important to emphasize that this unity is a spiritual union in Christ. It has absolutely nothing to do with our flesh and blood, nationality, custom, or culture. When the Bible says, "there is neither male nor female" that does not mean that a male is no longer a male and a female is no longer a female. A Greek is still a Greek, and a Jew continues to be a Jew. So the accusation we often hear from unbelievers that the Church is divided because there are so many different denominations is actually baseless. The Bible teaches perfect unity in Christ. Note the last sentence: "ye are all one in Christ Jesus." This idea really destroys the philosophy of the ecumenical system, and the many church-oriented, unity-seeking organizations that attempt to dissolve denominational borders. The differences that exist have no direct relationship to the Church of Jesus Christ.

To summarize, the closer I am to Jesus, the closer I will be to my brothers and sisters in the Lord. The unity does not need to exist in flesh and blood, which would be horizontal, but this unity already exists perfectly in a vertical fashion. What is the difference between horizontal and vertical fellowship? Horizontal fellowship means our ties to brothers and sisters in the Lord. This unity is not required because we exist on earth in our flesh and blood. Vertical fellowship is spiritual. That is the only relationship that really counts. In our spirit we are united in one faith to our Lord Jesus Christ who sits at the right hand of God.

Unity Must Be Anchored in Jesus

I have experienced this type of unity on many occasions when I travel to different countries. When we come together with other born-again believers, we don't ask which church or fellowship he or she attends — our unity in Jesus Christ is already perfectly one. Thus, our subject is the precious Word of God, the fulfillment of Bible prophecy, the imminent return of the Lord Jesus Christ, and the fact that our task on earth is almost complete.

Of course we should strive for unity, but the goal of our unity must be with one person only, the Lord Jesus Christ. The closer we are united in the Lord, serving Him with fear and trembling, the sweeter our fellowship with Him, and with each other, will be. Organizational unity is necessary for the Church to function but this type of unity must not be compared to the spiritual unity of the Church.

The "Perfect Man" Unity

Ephesians 4:13 is often misunderstood: "Till we all come in the unity of the faith, and of the knowledge of the Son of God, unto a perfect man, unto the measure of the stature of the fulness of Christ." When we quote only a portion of that Scripture, "Till we all come in the unity of the faith," we can justify the goal and work of the ecumenical movement and its associated groups, but this Scripture specifically emphasizes the individual person "unto a perfect man." What does this mean? True unity is not measured by how closely you are associated with your brother and sister organizationally or in the interpretation of doctrine, but true unity is growing in Christ "unto a perfect man."

This perfect unity of the Church of Jesus Christ is absolutely unique and cannot be imitated. Satan, however, wants to imitate God; thus, his goal is to establish a one-world church.

God is the originator of different nations, tongues, and people, "By these were the isles of the Gentiles divided in their lands; every one after his tongue, after their families, in their nations" (Genesis 10:5). He even divided the land into continents: "And unto Eber were born two sons: the name of one was Peleg; for in his days was the earth divided; and his brother's name was Joktan" (Genesis 10:25).

Therefore, the spirit of transnational, intercultural unity in today's world is contrary to God's will. The Church of Jesus Christ is connected to only one earthly people: Israel. The Church is God's heavenly people; the Jews are God's earthly people.

The world's humanistic unity will bring forth more prosperity, more comfort, and less chance of war, but it is obvious from Scripture that God has not intended for it to be that way — that unity can only take place on His terms!

CHAPTER 15

HOW WILL THE WORLD BECOME ONE?

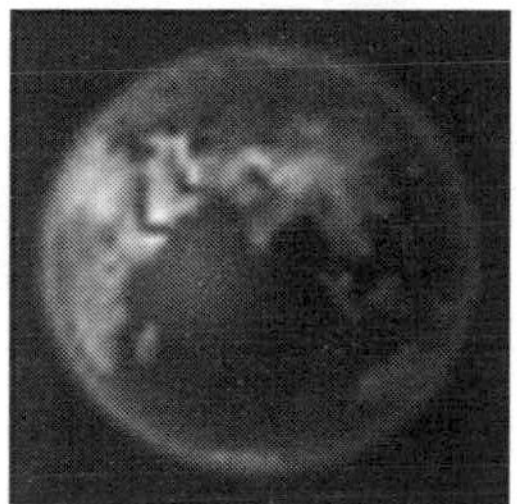

Democracy has produced the greatest forms of peace and prosperity the world has ever known and it will spread in a worldwide fashion under the Antichrist. Democracy will lead to the introduction of the Mark of the Beast, which the majority of the population will gladly accept as a path to increased peace, prosperity and security. We also discover that communism failed because of a lack of concern for money and we'll consider how credit cards are a first step toward the coming cashless society.

How Will the World Become One?

One of the most difficult things to grasp for citizens who have lived under a so-called free system such as democracy is that it will usher in the new age of the Antichrist; a temporary time of world peace and prosperity.

World unity is being accomplished in different ways and on different levels. An article from the April 26, 1992 edition of the *Kansas City Star* provides us with a glimpse of how world unity is coming together:

> A new economy rules. Because of their different histories and present circumstances, Japan and Europe will be infusing the capitalistic economy with strategies very different from those found in the Anglo-Saxon world.
>
> They will force the economic leaders of the 19th and 20th century, the United Kingdom and the United States, to alter the way they play the economic game.[35]

The new social/capital economy will incorporate different strategies and is indeed altering the traditional economic game the leaders of the world have played thus far.

What we see developing today is unprecedented. The success lies in rejecting the old traditional ways and pulling out onto new avenues to achieve prosperity, success and unity.

Britain first held the torch but the United States has

been the world's economic leader for most of the last century. If other nations tried to interfere, they were silenced by force.

For example, when the Dutch established New Amsterdam (today's New York), the British simply told them to get out and they had no choice but to obey. This type of power wielding was the norm in politics, economy, military and religion until the beginning of the 1900s.

As already mentioned, the United States is no longer the undisputed leader of the world. Our national debts testify against any other theory. Britain, once a world empire, is now one of the poorer nations in Europe. England's standard of living is substantially lower than that of Switzerland, Sweden, Germany, and Norway. So, just as was pointed out in the *Kansas City Star* article, the old Anglo-American system is failing and will be surpassed by the new social/capital world system now being developed in Europe.

The Coming European World

The new European power structure will fulfill the prophetic predictions that tell us that a one-world system will be implemented. Once the system is established, it will fall into the hands of an extremely clever person the Bible identifies as the Antichrist.

The fourth Gentile empire, which is being established today, does not need to be labeled as the

Roman Empire or the One-World Order. These and many other labels that are being coined today will ultimately merge into one.

Whether the unity of the world is promoted by certain organizations such as the Illuminati, Bilderbergers, the Club of Rome, the G-7, the United Nations, or any other, the aim and the result will be the same.

It is not necessary to distinguish between each of them and analyze their objectives because it is the same one-world spirit. The same spirit prompted the building of the Tower of Babel. We can justifiably call the movement toward world unity an unmistakable sign of the endtimes. The Antichrist will be especially successful in the last days when he incorporates the world into one.

Important for Christians to understand is that the progress and subsequent success of the new world is not necessarily evil and should not be rejected by believers, but we must always keep in mind that we are in the world and not of the world.

All Governments are Ordained by God

When we analyze the situation of the world, we must not forget that "there is no power [government] but of God: the powers that be are ordained of God" (Romans 13:1). When Christians become politically partial, then we are actively participating in the political process and become part of the world. I am fully aware that I will be chided for making such a statement, but I believe it is biblical.

Joseph was as a slave in a foreign government as was Esther. Daniel faithfully served two dictatorships that had destroyed his own country and led to his captivity. Above all else, Jesus was obedient to the dictatorship of Rome!

All governments have been ordained by God, but each and every one is placed under the jurisdiction of the devil because he is the god of this world. He is the prince of the powers of darkness. No doubt, there are great differences between the various governments, and surely, the communist governments committed more evil acts than the democratic governments, but these things have no direct relationship to the Church of Jesus Christ.

Using All Things Liberally

The Bible is clear that regardless of the world's evil condition, believers can make use of all things in our service to God. Thus, we read in 1 Corinthians 3:22: "Whether Paul, or Apollos, or Cephas, or the world, or life, or death, or things present, or things to come; all are yours." We may use all modern facilities, inventions and products to further the Gospel, and not feel like we have to analyze everything for hidden diabolic intent.

For example, we have had people tell us they will not subscribe to our magazine because we accept credit cards as forms of payment. These people assumed that we were in cahoots with the devil, but we would be blind if we denied that a one-world economy already existed.

New Currency

Much has been written about the proposed new money. While in many parts of the world new money is being issued rather frequently it is almost unthinkable in the United States. We have gotten used to the "greenback" over the last several generations. This is equally true for the British currency. Incidentally, both currencies are continuously losing purchasing power and financial experts have little doubt that the currencies will need to be replaced. The following is an interesting article in connection with this idea:

> The consequences of a universal currency will be simplicity of all arithmetic, operation and facilities gained for travelers, the easing of international transactions and the simplification of exchange rates. When we have a universal currency, trading will receive such a stimulus that it will bypass all the trade records experienced so far.[36]

Does that sound like some overly optimistic prediction? Wrong! This was written in 1870 by Mr. Feer Herzog, the Swiss Finance Minister in France. Already at that time, there were those who dreamed of a unified Europe and a united currency!

World Communism

What is especially unique today is the fact that the competing forces of capitalism and communism are being merged into one since the fall of international communism. The communist system could not compete with social/capitalism because it ignored monetary policy.

Back in 1967 Dr. Wim Malgo wrote an article in our first American edition of *Midnight Call* entitled, "Communism: Doomed to Fail." We have witnessed its collapse but it was unthinkable in 1967 because we had heard so much about the great communist threat. Russia was ahead of the United States in weapons production and space travel and she was swallowing up one country after another. The U.S. lost the war against the small nation of North Vietnam. The communists achieved one great victory after another in many parts of the world.

Why did communism fail? There were many reasons, but one specific point that I would like to mention here is that communism failed to consider that man is basically evil, selfish and money hungry. Capitalism, on the other hand, thrives on the love of money. A book entitled *Greed Is Good* was published during the Reagan administration.

Anti-God Communism

Communism revealed itself as being anti-God. The communist's motto was "God is dead!" When my mother-in-law was alive she frequently traveled behind the Iron Curtain to visit her relatives in communist East Germany. She always brought *Midnight Call* literature with her in spite of the fact that it was forbidden. She was caught with the literature several times but the authorities did not arrest her because of her age.

When in East Germany, Mom always took long walks in the fields of the countryside. On one occasion, she saw a large sign in a wheat field that the communists had put up that said, "*Ohne Gott und Sonnenschein bringen wir doch die Ernte ein!*" ("Without God and sunshine we will still bring the harvest in.") The communists challenged God. Their confidence was strengthened because they had just imported brand new grain harvesters from Russia, which were supposedly capable of harvesting wheat during wet seasons. Then one day it started to rain. This, of course was not unusual, but the rain continued for seven days. The result was predictable. The crop was flattened. They were unable to harvest the grain even with the most sophisticated Russian machinery. The billboards disappeared overnight. The communists had taken them down because they were embarrassed by their arrogance.

I don't have to tell you that my mother-in-law, who was a believer, praised the Lord, rejoicing in her heart to see these foolish people defeated by the mighty hand of God.

Anti-Christ Capitalist

The capitalistic system is not anti-God but anti-Christ. The system of capital democracy will usher in the Antichrist; therefore, I propose we watch it more carefully in our day.

Communism was based upon the productivity of the worker. Karl Marx, a German Jew, stated in 1848: "If the workers of the world unite, they will be able to bring forth a paradise on Earth." But communism failed because it was not centered on the love of money. Instead, they invented their own financial system that was not backed by personal incentives for the individual. Communism rejected that idea and developed the philosophy that all people are created equal, subsequently, they will remain equal.

A degree of greediness is essential in order to make a capitalistic economy work properly. People who seek personal wealth generally work a lot more than the average citizen. Many successful businessmen work between 12 and 16 hours a day. Some work six, even seven days a week. They think about profit and individual wealth all the time. They are dedicated to success and they love money.

Believers must learn a lesson here: we must also work day and night, but the work we do is of eternal value. Gold and silver perish, but precious souls that will be saved by the blood of the Lord Jesus Christ will remain forever. They will make up our crown of jewels, our reward for all of eternity.

We all need money. Midnight Call Ministries could not function without money. We must pay to print our magazines, books and tracts. We need money for wages, missionaries, and postage. We need money for just about everything. But money should only serve to sustain our standard of living, and most of all, to further the work of the Lord. That is the reason the Lord gives us health: so that we can work, earn money, and help to further the Gospel.

Ultimate Control

Money will play a major role in the coming one-world system. In the book of Revelation, we read: "And he causeth all, both small and great, rich and poor, free and bond, to receive a mark in their right hand, or in their foreheads: And that no man might buy or sell, save he that had the mark, or the name of the beast, or the number of his name" (Revelation 13:16-17). This is obviously the ultimate system for money control as far as the endtimes are concerned.

The Mark of the Beast, or the number of his name, will become a financial necessity. I do not believe, however, that this mark will be forced upon people. The general public will recognize the advantages this system provides and will gladly receive it.

It is significant that worship is mentioned first. The people who receive the Mark of the Beast will be convinced that this is the right thing to do because the system will eliminate many of the evils within our society.

Think about it: Tax fraud deepens our national debt and places more burden upon honest citizens. The drug trade would receive an immediate death blow. The evil deeds of drug dealers would stop because there would be no more cash. Virtually all cash-related crimes would stop. The majority of the people will gladly receive the Mark of the Beast for these and other obvious benefits.

Credit Cards: The First Step Toward Global Money

It is necessary today to have a credit card if you wish to travel, especially to foreign countries, as it would be very difficult to make hotel and airplane reservations without one. A credit card is the most economic and practical form of currency you can use in a foreign country. It will save you from having to go through the time consuming process of exchanging American dollars for local currency, not to mention the astronomical fees charged by the moneychangers.

We talked earlier about a global currency and pointed out that the credit card is the beginning of a unified currency. Unfortunately, someone could use it simply by forging your signature; therefore, it is almost natural that this system would have to develop further. A credit system that cannot be lost or stolen will offer itself as security for transactions — a permanent bodily mark! This global system will be the most successful financial/political/economic and religious system the world has ever known!

Just think for a moment about the amount of money

that could be saved by operating a one-world government with only one military force. Think about the tax cuts and the money freed up for more beneficial uses. It is for that reason the nations will gladly accept the Mark of the Beast with the new world ruler system that promises peace and prosperity on earth.

Eternal Unity

But while the world is being united and prepares to welcome the Antichrist, believers are "Looking for that blessed hope, and the glorious appearing of the great God and our Saviour Jesus Christ" (Titus 2:13). Christians are preparing for the coming of the Lord.

When Jesus cried out, "My God, my God, why hast thou forsaken me?" He had paid the price in full for the sins of all mankind. Calvary finished the payment for sin and unified all who believe.

Man's unity is based on his own intellectual capacity, which is tainted with sin and will lead to Armageddon.

Money is still the name of the game whether you are the richest man on earth or a homeless person. There is no difference at death, regardless of whether you are Sam Walton [founder of the Wal-Mart chain], who was called the richest man in the world, or the poor homeless fellow who lives underneath a bridge. The only thing that counts when you die is whether you trusted in the atoning sacrifice of Jesus Christ.

CHAPTER 16

DOOMSDAY PROPHECIES

"Clean up our earth," they insist. "Respect nature so that worldwide healing can begin." The errors of these and other beliefs have been addressed in this chapter. We will see how the world is being led to believe rumors instead of facts.

Let's look at the militant supporters of the environmental movement. Many of their claims regarding pollution are based on false information. We will document some of those beliefs.

Of course, there is a problem with pollution and trees are being cut down in greater volume but the fact that vegetation has increased, rivers and lakes are cleaner and our air is purer than it was 50 years ago is often not mentioned.

Some people believe that they will gain some sort of salvation on earth if they fight for a better world, cleaner air, purer water and more vegetation. Yet all manner of spiritual, moral and ethical pollution is tolerated, even encouraged.

I believe that this over-emphasized environmental movement is the devil's cover-up for the real problem man faces: sin.

Doesn't it seem strange that the world is so united when it comes to the ecological status of planet Earth, but they ignore the Creator?

The answer is probably found in the fact that most of these people are not Christians. They do not know about the hope of a heavenly home, and so they concern themselves only with the here and now.

Let's look at some false prophecies that have been made in recent years concerning the environment. An article that was printed in the January/February 1995 edition of *The Futurist* magazine opposed the alarmists by providing scientific answers to seven of the most popular lies about the environment. Keep in mind that *The Futurist* is not published by a religious organization; nevertheless, I would like to share the comments from this article with you:

Seven False Prophecies • 1 — Global Famine

"The battle to feed all of humanity is over. In the 1970's the world will undergo famines — hundreds of millions of people are going to starve to death in spite of any crash programs embarked upon now," predicted population alarmist Paul Ehrlich in his book, *The Population Bomb* (1968).

What really happened? While the world's population doubled since World War II, food production tripled. The real price of wheat and corn dropped by 60%, while the price of rice was cut in half.

Seven False Prophecies • 2 — Exhaustion of Nonrenewable Resources

In 1972, the Club of Rome's notorious report, *The Limits to Growth*, predicted that at exponential growth rates the world would run out of raw materials — gold by 1981, mercury by 1985, tin by 1987, zinc by 1990, oil by 1992, and copper, lead and natural gas by 1993.

What really happened? Humanity hasn't come close to running out of any mineral resource. Even the World Resources Institute estimates that the average price of all metals and minerals fell by more than 40% between 1970 and 1988. As we all know, falling prices mean that goods are becoming more abundant, not more scarce.

Seven False Prophecies • 3 — Skyrocketing Pollution

In 1972, *The Limits to Growth* also predicted that pollution would skyrocket as population and industry increased: "Virtually every pollutant that has been measured as a function of time appears to be increasing exponentially."

What really happened? Since the publication of *The Limits to Growth*, U.S. population has risen 22% and the economy has grown by more than 58%. Yet, instead of increasing as predicted, air pollutants have dramatically declined.

Sulfur dioxide emissions are down 25% and carbon monoxide down 41%. Volatile organic compounds — chief contributors to smog formation — have been reduced by 31%, and total particulates like smoke, soot, and dust have fallen by 59%. Smog dropped by 50% in Los Angeles over the last decade.

Seven False Prophecies • 4 — The Coming Ice Age

The public has forgotten that the chief climatological threat being hyped by the eco-doomsters in the 1970's was the beginning of a new ice age. The new ice age was allegedly the result of mankind's polluting haze, which was blocking sunlight.

What really happened? Global temperatures, after declining for 40 years, rebounded in the late 1970's, averting the feared new ice age. But was this cause for rejoicing? NO! Now we are supposed to fear global warming. Freeze or fry, the problem is always viewed as industrial capitalism, and the solution, international socialism.

Seven False Prophecies • 5 — Antarctic Ozone Hole

There have been widespread fears that the hole in the

ozone layer of the Earth's atmosphere will wipe out life all over the world. John Lynch, program manager of polar aeronomy at the National Science Foundation, declared in 1989, "It's terrifying. If these ozone holes keep growing like this, they'll eventually eat the world."

What really happened? In 1985, British scientists detected reduced levels of stratospheric ozone over Antarctica. Could the Antarctic ozone hole "eventually eat the world"? No, "It is a purely localized phenomenon," according to Guy Brasseur at the National Center for Atmospheric Research. It is thought that the "ozone hole" results from catalytic reactions of some chlorine-based chemicals, which can take place only in high, very cold (below -80C, or -176F) clouds in the presence of sunlight. It is a transitory phenomenon enduring only a bit more than a month in the astral spring.

Seven False Prophecies • 6 — Ozone Hole Over U.S.A.

In 1992, NASA spooked Americans by declaring that an ozone hole like the one over Antarctica could open up over the United States. *Time* magazine showcased the story on its front cover (February 16, 1992), warning that "danger is shining through the sky... No longer is the threat just to our future; the threat is here and now." Then-Senator Albert Gore thundered in Congress, "We have to tell our children that they must redefine their relationship to the sky, and they must begin to think of the sky as a threatening part of their environment."

What really happened? On April 30, 1992, NASA sheepishly admitted that no ozone hole had opened up over the United States. *Time*, far from trumpeting the news on its cover, buried the admission in four lines of text in its May 11 issue. It's no wonder the American public is frightened.

Seven False Prophecies • 7 — Global Warming

Global warming is "The Mother of all environmental scares," according to the late political scientist Aaron Wildavsky. Based on climate computer models, eco-doomsters predict that the Earth's average temperature will increase by 4-9 degrees Fahrenheit over the next century due to the "greenhouse effect."

Burning fossil fuels boosts atmospheric carbon dioxide, which traps the sun's heat.

What is really happening? The Earth's average temperature has apparently increased by less than a degree (0.9) Fahrenheit in the last century. And here's more bad news for doomsters: Fifteen years of very precise satellite data show that the planet has actually cooled by 0.13 degrees C.[37]

How Lies are Used To Deceive the Masses

False prophecies, rumors, imagination and gossip generate their own energy but ultimately experience a burnout. These doomsday prophecies are Satan's clever attempt to divert man's attention from the real doomsday: the Great Tribulation that is going to come upon the earth.

God has been banned from our public places. Bible reading and prayer are no longer allowed in our schools. Thus, people are worshiping the creation more than the Creator. Romans 1:25 mentions those, "Who changed the truth of God into a lie, and worshiped and served the creature more than the Creator, who is blessed for ever. Amen."

We are seeing large numbers of the world's population worship nature, trees and animals instead of the living God. New Agers look inward and adopt an age-old religion: they believe that they are God.

The coming catastrophe will not be spurred on by environmental issues, it will, however, be the result of man's refusal to obey the Word of God and his belief in Satan's lies.

Should Christians "Stand Up"?

Unlike the environmentalist who believes in saving this world, discerning Christians are not waiting for the world to get better because we know that the Bible does not contain such a teaching. We are not deluded by the absurd notion that Christians will eventually take over the government, the legislatures and courts. Discerning Christians realize we have not been given a biblical calling to "stand up" in the name of Jesus and politically oppose wickedness in public places. We have been called to preach the Gospel and call sinners to repentance and salvation. We are waiting for the Lord Jesus Christ to take us OUT of this world and to live with Him forevermore!

Peter's Admonition is Good for Us Today

We will close this chapter with 2 Peter 3:11-18:

Seeing then that all these things shall be dissolved, what manner of persons ought ye to be in all holy conversation and godliness, Looking for and hasting unto the coming of the day of God, wherein the heavens being on fire shall be dissolved, and the elements shall melt with fervent heat? Nevertheless we, according to his promise, look for new heavens and a new earth, wherein dwelleth righteousness. Wherefore, beloved, seeing that ye look for such things, be diligent that ye may be found of him in peace, without spot, and blameless. And account that the longsuffering of our Lord is salvation; even as our beloved brother Paul also according to the wisdom given unto him hath written unto you; As also in all his epistles, speaking in them of these things; in which are some things hard to be understood, which they that are unlearned and unstable wrest, as they do also the other scriptures, unto their own destruction. Ye therefore, beloved, seeing ye know these things before, beware lest ye also, being led away with the error of the wicked, fall from your own stedfastness. But grow in grace, and in the knowledge of our Lord and Saviour Jesus Christ. To him be glory both now and for ever. Amen.

CHAPTER 17

DEMOCRACY: GOD OF THE NEW AGE

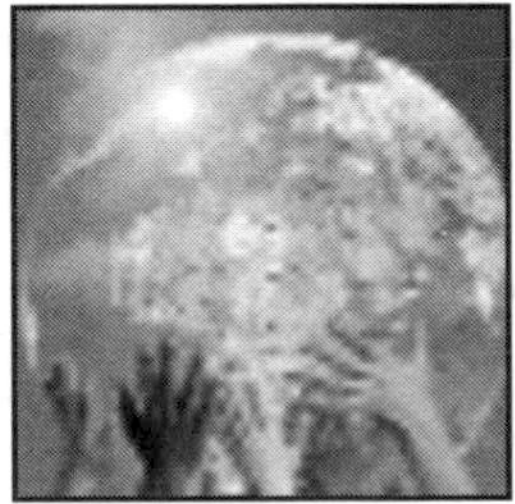

Recent victories of democracy have opened the door for world unity. If democracy is the final system of the Gentiles, will it install the Antichrist? How must Christians relate to the coming one-world democracy?

Democracy: God of the New Age

I know that the title of this chapter will be controversial. It may sound as if I am putting democracy down, but that is not my intention. We have experienced democracy as a political system that works best at this moment. Democracy provides certain unprecedented freedoms. At this time, there is no other viable system that can compare to democracy, but as we analyze the system from a biblical perspective, we will find that democracy, no matter how good, will ultimately install the Antichrist.

The fact that we are experiencing a flood of democracy today gives us more reason than ever to believe that the conclusion of the endtimes is indeed at hand.

Democracy is on the lips of everyone today, especially since the unexpected sensational fall of the Iron Curtain. Not one day passes without some report by the news media about the progress of democracy. Some have called democracy the ultimate freedom and liberty for mankind. Others say democracy is the God-given right of everyone on earth.

Goddess of Democracy

Democracy is considered a religion in communist China. A papier mache´ Statue of Liberty was displayed during the Chinese student uprising in Tiananmen Square. It was called the "Goddess of Democracy." I would like to address this point in detail because a god or goddess of democracy can never be the God of the Bible that we worship.

Think about it for a moment. Children educated in communism rebelled against the system. They had to be good communists, otherwise, they would not have been allowed to study at a Chinese university. Yet, these students were the ones who put up this "Goddess of Democracy" sign. Did they recognize something that we as a nation have not? I think so!

We published an article in this connection in the July 1989 issue of *News from Israel,* which I will quote in part:

> The hope for democracy and the tragedy that followed has been publicized by the news media in detail. What is the significance from the prophetic Word? Geographically, China lies directly east of Israel. Its participation in the endtime scenario is described for us in Revelation 16:12, "And the sixth angel poured out his vial upon the great river Euphrates; and the water thereof was dried up, that the way of the kings of the east might be prepared."
>
> Although China is a communist country, they separated themselves from Soviet communism under the leadership of Mao Tse Tung. This did not come as a surprise to students of the Scripture, because China is not categorized within the northern confederacy mentioned by the prophet Ezekiel in chapters 38 and 39. China belongs to the confederacy of kings of the East and therewith to the world empire, which is presently arising in Europe.

> While the uprisings in the former Soviet bloc countries were based exclusively on materialistic and nationalistic reasons, the uprising in China is different because it includes a religious fervor, as clearly expressed in the "Goddess of Democracy."[38]

Democracy on the March

In the meantime, we have witnessed the fall of the Berlin Wall, a symbol that separated East from West, communism from capitalism. Now, as we witness democracy move East rather than communism move West, as was feared for so long, it is considered the bottom line to all the world's problems.

Who can stand in the way of democracy? Just a few years ago, communism was perhaps the most powerful system in the world. Geographically, over half of our planet and about 65 percent of the world's population was ruled by it.

Now democracy has the center stage since this threat to capitalist freedom no longer poses any real danger. It is the new world power of today. We are approaching the time when no one will be able to oppose democracy.

Here we are reminded of Revelation 13:4: "Who is like unto the beast? who is able to make war with him?"

While we rejoice that our brothers and sisters in the Lord in Eastern Europe can gather more freely in fellowship, and we are happy for the liberty they now have to travel to the West, we must not allow this joy to blind us to the new danger that is approaching. The danger that actually seems so positive is a united world under democracy.

But who in his right mind could oppose such progress? What's wrong with universal brotherhood, global unity, peace and prosperity? On the surface, nothing, but those who diligently study the Scripture know exactly where this development will lead.

Since the beginning of time, men have been waiting for the right person with the right system that would lead to universal peace and harmony, but men have wanted it on their own terms. Is peace and prosperity a realistic possibility in our time? Yes! Not only is peace possible but it must come because it is prophesied in Holy Scripture. Yes, there will be peace at an unprecedented level and it will flood the world in such a way that all opposition will be eliminated.

At the zenith of success, however, it will assume a different face. The gloves will come off and its true nature will be revealed. No longer will it move only horizontally, that is, globally, but it will begin to move vertically because men want to be God.

Democracy Cannot Change the Evil Heart

The success of democracy is based on human intellect, but men will be just as wicked as ever: "The heart is deceitful above all things, and desperately wicked: who can know it?" (Jeremiah 17:9).

Bible readers are familiar with the altercation that took place between Cain and Abel. An argument arose and one man killed the other. Since that time, brother has waged war against brother. We can be certain that this type of conflict will continue. Wars and rumors of wars, arguments, dissatisfaction, and rebellion will not cease until Jesus returns. Only He can bring about true peace.

Regardless of the system of the world's governments, all have promised a peaceful and improved life. The goal of virtually all politicians has never changed: they have always assured the people, in effect, "Peace and prosperity for our people, if you elect me."

If that is true, then why have there been so many wars? War is based on hatred. This hatred has not been done away with. It is still engrained deep in the heart of every single person on earth, unless that person has been bought with the blood of the Lamb, the Lord Jesus Christ. Only then will that individual have real peace that passes all understanding, and will be able to overcome the hatred that so saturates the human heart and mind.

Democratic Dictatorship

The danger of democracy lies in the ironic fact that it will ultimately not tolerate any opposition. The new world democracy of the last days will become, in effect, a world dictatorship.

We found the following in the "Popular Quotations" section of *Webster's Encyclopedic Dictionary of the English Language*: Democracy means simply the bludgeoning of the people, by the people, for the people.

The point I want to make is that the intoxicating joy that is being expressed today due to the success of democracy is actually no reason to rejoice:

> And I saw three unclean spirits like frogs come out of the mouth of the dragon, and out of the mouth of the beast, and out of the mouth of the false prophet. For they are the spirits of devils, working miracles, which go forth unto the kings of the earth and of the whole world, to gather them to the battle of that great day of God Almighty (Revelation 16:13-14).

The "unclean spirits" are at work today throughout the world. For the first time in the history of mankind it has become possible for a world system to be implemented in order to fulfill Bible prophecy, which clearly reveals that the world will unite. But that is not the final goal. In the end, a united world will prepare for battle against God.

This is not visible today. No one is talking about fighting God. No one in his right mind would even suggest such a thought, but the Scripture we have just read plainly states that the miraculous works accomplished by the nations will have a specific aim: the gathering union against God Almighty.

The Christian's Battle

Today more than ever, Christians must make sure that their position is that of spectators looking over the political field, not down on the turf fighting it out with the pagans. Our goal is to serve the risen and exalted Lord, spread the liberating Gospel, and prepare ourselves for His return.

We must not debase ourselves by being drawn into things that belong to the world. We must not believe that we are in charge, and that through our activity we can produce world peace, justice and freedom.

We know with certainty that God controls the world. He installs presidents, prime ministers, kings, and other officials; therefore, our battle is supremely more important than merely controlling or influencing a political system. Because our battle is distinctly not with flesh and blood, the Apostle Paul wrote, "For we wrestle not against flesh and blood, but against principalities, against powers, against the rulers of the darkness of this world, against spiritual wickedness in high places" (Ephesians 6:12).

CHAPTER 18

THE TIME OF THE GENTILES AND ISRAEL

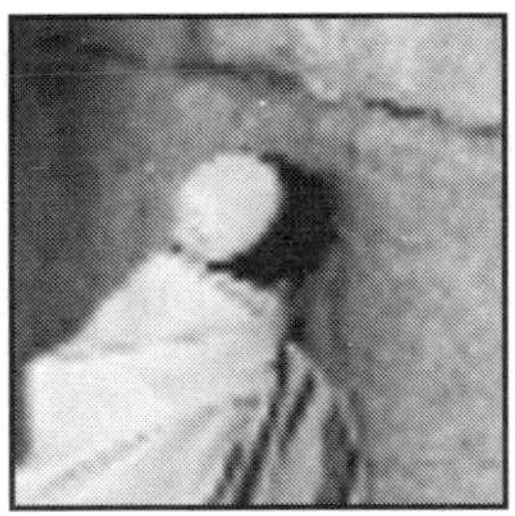

The rise of the last Gentile world empire is a sign by which we can recognize that we are living in the end stages of the endtimes. The nations are beginning to establish their own world society of peace and prosperity through social democracy but God is making His own preparation for real peace and the establishment of the coming Millennium.

The Time of the Gentiles

The endtimes began about 2,600 years ago when the first world empire was founded. Daniel made this point clear when he wrote: "Thou, O king, art a king of kings: for the God of heaven hath given thee a kingdom, power, and strength, and glory" (Daniel 2:37).

God used the Babylonian King Nebuchadnezzar to provide us with a picture of the four empires. And the fourth, which is the last, reaches to the end to time. As we have previously mentioned, we are seeing the implementation of the last Gentile power structure take place today.

After Daniel described the four world empires, which were revealed in Nebuchadnezzar's dream, we read, "And in the days of these kings shall the God of heaven set up a kingdom, which shall never be destroyed: and the kingdom shall not be left to other people, but it shall break in pieces and consume all these kingdoms, and it shall stand for ever" (Daniel 2:44). Incidentally, this verse should eliminate all time-based speculation. What these few words say is that God has been establishing His kingdom for the last 2,600 years and it will be manifested in, with and through Israel. Once that has been established the law will go out from Jerusalem and all the world will have to obey because the Lord will then rule with a rod of iron.

We see the picture start to come together: God is about to set up His kingdom but He cannot establish the kingdom parallel to the one in which the world is building, thus, the governments, their systems, and all world political identities must be done away with.

Israel Must Be Resurrected

At the same time, it was absolutely necessary that Israel be established as an independent nation on the soil promised to their forefathers. The purpose of Israel's establishment is listed in the next verse: "Forasmuch as thou sawest that the stone was cut out of the mountain without hands, and that it brake in pieces the iron, the brass, the clay, the silver, and the gold; the great God hath made known to the king what shall come to pass hereafter: and the dream is certain, and the interpretation thereof sure" (Daniel 2:45). One thing is clear: the stone, which is the rock of salvation, the Lord Jesus Christ, came from Israel. He must return there because He is the very stone that is the threshing instrument of judgment to be used against the nations.

Furthermore, Israel has been given to us as an example. In 1 Corinthians 10:6 we read, "Now these things were our examples." So, whatever has happened in the past is an example to us so that we may see and recognize the times in which we live.

God's eternal plan of redemption is to offer personal salvation to the individual, through an individual, His only begotten Son, the Lord Jesus

Christ. God's eternal plan of salvation also calls for the liberation of the nations.

Liberation from what? Liberation from dictatorship, monarchy, nationalism, communism, and even democracy. This will be accomplished through the nation of Israel.

Unfulfilled Peace

The coming Messiah was the promise for Israel: "And he [Jesus] shall reign over the house of Jacob for ever; and of his kingdom there shall be no end" (Luke 1:33). In spite of this promise, however, Israel is still not saved, and the world still has no peace! The promise of Scripture is clear: "on earth peace, good will toward men" (Luke 2:14). And in verse 10, we read: "I bring you good tidings of great joy, which shall be to all people." Indeed, we must admit that this heavenly message has not yet been fulfilled on earth. There is no peace on earth, good will toward men, or great joy, at least not among the nations. Men continue to fight, argue, and debate; thus, we know that this part of prophecy will have to be fulfilled in the future.

Fulfilled Promise

Read the promise the Lord Jesus Christ made to His disciples, and therewith to us, in John 14:27: "Peace I leave with you, my peace I give unto you: not as the world giveth, give I unto you. Let not your heart be troubled, neither let it be afraid." And John 16:33: "These things I have spoken unto you, that in me ye might have peace. In the world ye shall have tribulation: but be of good cheer; I have overcome the world."

Praise God! What a message! The most important thing we need to worry about is our personal relationship with Him — everything else is secondary! Philippians 4:7 promises: "And the peace of God, which passeth all understanding, shall keep your hearts and minds through Christ Jesus." Personal peace is available — national peace is not.

Manmade Peace

Now that we have seen the kind of peace God gives, we may ask, "What's wrong with man's attempt toward peace? Is it against God's will for men to bring about peace and live in fellowship and harmony with one another? Are we not admonished in the Bible to live peacefully with one another? Does the Scripture not say, "Blessed are the peacemakers" (Matthew 5:9)? While that is all true, the peace that is being produced by man has no relationship to the peace that was brought about by God. Man's peace is temporary. It is not real because man did not pay the ultimate price to obtain it. God is peace. Man sinned against God; thus, man could no longer claim peace. Subsequently, any human attempts to repair the damage will fail. We can better understand

Ephesians 2:14 in this light: "For he is our peace, who hath made both one, and hath broken down the middle wall of partition between us."

Tower of Babel Democracy

The first attempt at peace through democracy is recorded in Genesis 11:4. No dictator was present nor do we read that a king gave a command. The builders of the Tower of Babel were "We the people." They were in charge of their affairs: "And they said one to another, Go to, let us make brick, and burn them thoroughly. And they had brick for stone, and slime had they for morter. And they said, Go to, let us build us a city and a tower, whose top may reach unto heaven; and let us make us a name, lest we be scattered abroad upon the face of the whole earth" (Genesis 11:3-4). Democracy was at work! God confused the languages of the people who were building the Tower of Babel because they wanted to unite themselves against God. They were united in their desire to make a name for themselves, not wanting to be scattered upon the face of the earth. Yet God had specifically instructed the people that they should scatter abroad and "replenish the earth." Thus, they acted contrary to the will of God.

Religion was the deeper motivation for the unity-minded builders of the Tower of Babel, "let us build us a city and a tower whose top may reach unto heaven" (Genesis 11:4). This is a clear indication that religion, "whose top may reach unto heaven" was the key in the building of the Tower of Babel. But man is incapable of building a way to heaven. God already accomplished it, but in the reverse direction — not from earth to heaven, but from heaven to earth. Thus, God had to stop the building of the Tower of Babel. He confused the languages and the construction business went bust. They had to leave off in their attempt to finish that tower. Instead they were forced to fulfill God's commandment to "replenish the earth."

Calling of One Man

What happened immediately after this episode of democracy in action at the Tower of Babel? God called Abraham. The Bible refers to Abraham as "the father of all them that believe." God separated Abraham from his family and nation and made a promise to him that was passed down to Isaac and Jacob, who was renamed Israel. Thus we see that God made it clear from the beginning that He is against world unity: not integration, but segregation. God segregated Abraham from the rest of the world.

In a remarkable way, the tiny nation of Israel, which consisted only of 70 of Abraham's descendants, moved to Egypt where they prospered and increased. It is apparent from Scripture that the Israelites knew about the blessings and promises God made to Abraham, Isaac and Jacob.

Segregation Not Integration

Also remarkable is the fact that Israel did not integrate with the Egyptians while they were still free. But when a new pharaoh had come to power he made sure that the Israelites would be separated from Egypt. He forced them into slavery. Here again we recognize God's master plan for Israel: not integration, but segregation!

Israel experienced a long period of oppression. We find no recorded evidence during that time regarding the divine workings of God among His people until Moses came along. Nevertheless, God had everything in His control.

Four hundred years after the promise to Abraham, God commanded Pharaoh through His servant Moses to let His people go. The Bible records the miracles God performed through the hand of Moses in the presence of Pharaoh to cause him to let Israel go. Ten terrible plagues came upon the land. With the fourth one, God acted decisively to assure segregation: "And I will sever in that day the land of Goshen, in which my people dwell, that no swarms of flies shall be there; to the end thou mayest know that I am the LORD in the midst of the earth. And I will put a division between my people and thy people: to morrow shall this sign be" (Exodus 8:22-23).

Segregation by Blood

The distinction between Israel and Egypt became

even more apparent when the tenth and final plague was to be executed upon Egypt:

> And all the firstborn in the land of Egypt shall die, from the firstborn of Pharaoh that sitteth upon his throne, even unto the firstborn of the maidservant that is behind the mill; and all the firstborn of beasts. And there shall be a great cry throughout all the land of Egypt, such as there was none like it, nor shall be like it any more. But against any of the children of Israel shall not a dog move his tongue, against man or beast: that ye may know how that the LORD doth put a difference between the Egyptians and Israel (Exodus 11:5-7).

This is obviously a distinct pronunciation of God's intention for mankind as well: not democracy, but theocracy; not unity, but segregation!

Proof of God Does Not Create Faith

We can barely imagine all the mighty miracles Israel experienced by the hand of God through His servant Moses. Egypt was judged and Israel was saved. The Israelites crossed the Red Sea on dry ground. They were fed quail and manna from heaven in the desert. They drank water from the rock at Mount Horeb. Then there was the defeated enemy, the powerful Amalekites, and the mighty miracle of God's audible voice from Mt. Sinai! Without a shadow of a doubt, God repeatedly demonstrated to Israel that He is the Almighty. And yet, Israel continued to rebel, and to disbelieve the Word of God!

Today we hear people say, "If I could have seen the mighty miracles God did at that time then I would believe." No, you would not believe. Israel didn't believe. If we saw all those miracles, it would only strengthen our flesh and blood, but in the spirit, we would remain empty and dry. We have the written Word, the Bible. It is God's action. We can see, experience, and test it for ourselves.

The full council of God is contained in the 66 books of the Bible. We don't need any additional revelation or miracles to confirm God's love. The Bible says, "Now faith is the substance of things hoped for, the evidence of things not seen" (Hebrews 11:1). The Bible also says, "For he that cometh to God must believe that he is" (Hebrews 11:6). Thus, there is no room for us to seek miracles or supernatural events to confirm our faith because "faith cometh by hearing...the Word of God" (Romans 10:17).

God lamented over those who had seen His mighty miracles and yet did not believe, nor did they obey His Word: "Because all those men which have seen my glory, and my miracles, which I did in Egypt and in the wilderness, and have tempted me now these ten times, and have not hearkened to my voice" (Numbers 14:22).

Seducing Miracles

People are seeking miracles today. This is why there

is so much deception in these endtimes. Many people claim to be the recipients of special visions and prophecies but I believe they are often demonically camouflaged in Christian terminology.

Matthew chapter 7 documents the shocking truth about a group of people who cast out demons and did mighty works in His name, yet the Lord said, "I know you not...ye workers of iniquity" (Luke 13:27).

I cannot overstate the fact that we must believe in the Lord Jesus Christ according to Scripture, "He that believeth on me, as the scripture hath said, out of his belly shall flow rivers of living water" (John 7:38).

I know better than to denounce or reject miracles. I am just warning that in these endtimes, especially before the Antichrist appears, Bible prophecy says there will be mighty signs and miracles performed by the spirit from below to confuse and to deceive mankind. The Scripture admonishes us to believe by faith rather than by sight: "Whom having not seen, ye love; in whom, though now ye see him not, yet believing, ye rejoice with joy unspeakable and full of glory" (1 Peter 1:8).

Only Moses Believed

In spite of God's tremendous acts, which the people of Israel experienced, they never consistently believed. David wrote, "He made known his ways unto Moses, his acts unto the children of Israel"

(Psalm 103:7). Then in Psalm 106:7 he confirms, "Our fathers understood not thy wonders in Egypt; they remembered not the multitude of thy mercies; but provoked him at the sea, even at the Red sea." None of the miracles Israel experienced strengthened their faith in God, but furthered them along the pathway of rebellion. Therefore, the unbelievers were forbidden to enter the Promised Land.

While their fathers perished in the desert, the children who entered the Promised Land eventually backslid as well: "Then all the elders of Israel gathered themselves together, and came to Samuel unto Ramah, And said unto him, Behold, thou art old, and thy sons walk not in thy ways: now make us a king to judge us like all the nations" (1 Samuel 8:4-5). Please note that all the elders came together. Apparently this was a perfect majority. Any politician would wish to have such support today!

"We the People..."

First Samuel 8 contains an account of blatant rebellion against the living God: "Then all the elders of Israel gathered themselves together." "We the people want to choose our own king," they said in effect. It was a simple request. "Make us a king to judge us like all the nations." They did not want to be separated from the heathen but desired to be like them.

When we read of this event in 1 Samuel, we notice that God didn't oppose this democratic process, He actually agreed to it. He gave the following commandment to Samuel: "Hearken unto the voice of the people in all that they say unto thee: for they have not rejected thee, but they have rejected me, that I should not reign over them" (1 Samuel 8:7). God knew where this would lead. He knew that Israel wanted to have its own way.

Israel's Quest for Gentile Democracy

In Moses' time, God gathered His people Israel: "And Moses brought forth the people out of the camp to meet with God; and they stood at the nether part of the mount" (Exodus 19:17). They had to come out of the camp and meet at a certain place to hear God's law. They heard the law but did not believe!

To summarize, Israel continuously rejected God's rule. Even though they experienced a multitude of miracles, they still said "No!" to the supreme rule of God. What a great tragedy!

But even after Israel's suffering under the ruler of foreign occupation, the people still rejected theocracy. In John 19:15, we read these very significant and yet sad words, "We have no king but Caesar." It was democracy in action once again. The multitude rose up against the Lord Jesus Christ. By this action, Israel said yes to the Roman Empire, and thereby to the revived Roman Empire of today — the European Union!

When we read about the crucifixion of Jesus we also see that the majority rules principle — the cardinal principle of democracy — was at work even during that time. The Roman politician Pilate confessed, "I find no fault in this man." Neither could the cruel King Herod accuse Jesus of any wrong-doing. After Jesus returned from Herod's presence, Pilate said, "I, having examined him before you, have found no fault in this man touching those things whereof ye accuse him: No, nor yet Herod: for I sent you to him; and, lo, nothing worthy of death is done unto him" (Luke 23:14-15). However, these two powerful politicians were overruled by democracy. Thus, we see that although majority rule may be preferred, it does not guarantee the execution of righteousness.

Israel Wants Integration

Israel's attempt to be like the Gentiles continues until this day. We know from Scripture that this desire will ultimately be fulfilled when Israel is integrated into the European Union — the last Roman Empire.

When analyzing Israel's history and future we must remember that Jesus prophesied: "If another shall come in his own name, him ye will receive" (John 5:43).

The following is an excerpt from page 24 of the May 1995 issue of *Midnight Call*:

Israel: One Step Closer To E.U.

Israel appears to be a step closer to associate status in the

European Union after France announced it would support opening E.U. research and development projects to Israeli firms on the same terms given to European companies.

Israel is seeking to upgrade its 1975 trade and economic agreement with the European body by asking for the same associate status as that given to Switzerland and Iceland, which provides economic benefits similar to regular E.U. membership but without voting rights. The E.U. has adopted a friendlier attitude toward Israel since the signing of the Declaration of Principles, particularly in the areas of research and development and agricultural imports.

Israeli Foreign Minister Shimon Peres, in Bonn for meetings with German officials, said if Israel opens its market to Palestinian agricultural products, it is only just that Israel should be compensated.

According to the Jewish Telegraphic Agency, Israel currently has a $5 billion trade deficit with the E.U., its main trading partner.[39]

The Coming False Peace

Israel's population is composed mainly of Jews from around the world. Their intellectual capacity as a nation is unsurpassed, but for the sake of peace and prosperity Israel takes great risks by accommodating former sworn enemies into a peace process on paper. Peace is the key word.

If peace can be brought about by these various processes of negotiation, then Israel will come closer to accepting the Antichrist, whom I believe will be a

Jewish person with an amazing ability to unite diverse factions, particularly Jews and Arabs.

Fundamentally, the Arabs hate the Jews because they received the promise of God and the Arabs did not. God chose the Jews for a specific purpose. The Lord Jesus said, "Salvation is of the Jews" (John 4:22).

A Forerunner of the Antichrist

Let us now analyze the person of the Antichrist. During the 30s and 40s, Germany experienced what I believe was the leadership of a forerunner of the Antichrist when Hitler was in power. The first six years of his leadership were a stunning success. Germany stood on its feet and unleashed an industrial powerhouse from out of hopelessness, depression and oppression. The Germans fully utilized an amazing pool of intellectuals, business people, and craftsmen. Almost naturally, all opposition was eliminated through the democratic process, which resulted in peace, prosperity, and success. The beginning of the downfall became visible only in the midst of Hitler's 12-year rule.

The Success of Antichrist

Don't expect the Antichrist to be an evil man with blood dripping from his mouth to appear on the world scene fomenting destruction and chaos. Rather, he will be a gentle, kind, compassionate, caring personality who is dedicated to true democracy and is determined to bring peace and prosperity to the world.

I can imagine that he will support prayer and Bible reading in schools, the political platform of the conservatives, and with a unique ability, he will appease the liberal camp as well. He will be all things to all people. Finally, the world will have a leader capable of taking care of all situations. Most importantly, he will prosper. His policies will actually work and not be empty political promises as our politicians are so fond of making today. He will accomplish great things!

Nevertheless, the Antichrist's work will be the work of darkness; the Lord's work is the work of light. He will destroy the Antichrist with the brightness of His coming, "the Lord shall consume with the spirit of his mouth, and shall destroy with the brightness of his coming" (2 Thessalonians 2:8). But all of the Antichrist's efforts will appear successful until the middle of the Tribulation.

On the Roman Road

One of the first steps toward peace for Israel must be taken in the direction of Rome. Peace will be virtually assured the day Israel is accepted into the European Union. Reuters news agency reported the following on December 29, 1993:

> In a landmark step after 2,000 years of strained Christian-Jewish relations, Vatican and Israeli negotiators approved a document in which the Holy See and the Jewish state formally recognize each other.
>
> The document, the most important step in Israeli-Vatican relations since the Jewish state was founded in 1948, was given final approval by delegations which had worked on the accord for 17 months.
>
> Vatican spokesman Joaquin Navarro-Valls said the accord may make it easier for the Vatican to play a greater role in constructing Middle East peace. In the preamble, the Vatican and Israel agree on the singular character and universal significance of the Holy Land.
>
> But in one important article, the Vatican states that while the Catholic Church reserves the right to speak out on moral issues, it agrees not to become directly involved in conflicts.
>
> The agreement says this principle applies specifically to "disputed territories and unsettled borders."
>
> In the same article, both sides commit themselves to support peaceful resolutions to local or world conflicts and to condemn terrorism.
>
> In another article, both sides agree to combat anti-semitism, racism, and religious intolerance. The Vatican states it deplores attacks on Jews, desecration of synagogues and cemeteries and acts which offend the memory of the victims of the Holocaust. Both sides agree to protect freedom of worship and respect each religion's sacred places.

> Israel recognizes the Catholic Church's right to run its own schools, communications media and welfare agencies in the Jewish state.[40]

The Power of Money

The amazing success of the new world system demonstrated uniquely through the European Union was brought to light when West Germany went across the border to East Germany and literally bought the country for cash! Many predicted doom and gloom, unemployment and a possible collapse of Germany's economy. Although unemployment did reach threatening proportions, the German mark stood strong, inflation was under control and the economy was healthy. These events, which are taking shape today, are unprecedented. Money, merchandise, and monopoly have become the strongest of forces and the world can no longer oppose them.

Israel will be Deceived

Israel cannot exist without becoming a part of the last world empire. The country must join itself with the mighty, money-oriented, social/democratic system. Finally, Israel will experience peace and prosperity. Until when? We read the answer in Daniel 11:36-39:

> And the king shall do according to his will; and he shall exalt himself, and magnify himself above every god, and shall

> speak marvellous things against the God of gods, and shall prosper till the indignation be accomplished: for that that is determined shall be done. Neither shall he regard the God of his fathers, nor the desire of women, nor regard any god: for he shall magnify himself above all. But in his estate shall he honour the God of forces: and a god whom his fathers knew not shall he honour with gold, and silver, and with precious stones, and pleasant things. Thus shall he do in the most strong holds with a strange god, whom he shall acknowledge and increase with glory: and he shall cause them to rule over many, and shall divide the land for gain.

That is the work of the Antichrist. He will come into power through deception and democracy.

The Time of Jacob's Trouble

But Israel will finally understand what is happening. The awakening will come when she sees the Antichrist in the temple and he declares that he is divine, "Who opposeth and exalteth himself above all that is called God, or that is worshipped; so that he as God sitteth in the temple of God, shewing himself that he is God" (2 Thessalonians 2:4).

At that time, God will act on behalf of His own people. Israel will suddenly realize that she has absolutely no hope and is lost. Then God will initiate His salvation, "And at that time shall Michael stand up, the great prince which standeth for the children of thy people: and there shall be a time of trouble, such as never was since there was a nation even to that same time: and at that time thy people shall be delivered, every one that shall be found written in the book" (Daniel 12:1).

That is the beginning of Israel's national salvation. For the first time in history an entire nation will be saved. Finally, the Jews will have learned that they cannot save themselves. Salvation must come from a higher authority, which is not democracy, but theocracy; not from man, but from God. This salvation will encompass all of Israel.

A Word of Invitation

In the meantime, God is still shouting this message through His servants, in effect saying, "Come to Jesus and be saved!" You must accept the Lord Jesus and His precious blood for the forgiveness of your sins. Nothing else will help you.

As we see these things come to pass — the one-world system being formed, the Roman Empire resurrected through the European Union, and the nations of the world gathering together against Israel — we know that we are living in the end stages of the endtimes.

The new age has already begun. It is the age that will deceive the entire world with peace, prosperity and democracy.

CHAPTER 19

THE GREAT TRIBULATION AND THE DAY OF THE LORD

Two-thirds of the world's population will be killed during the Great Tribulation. No one will be able to exist without the Mark of the Beast. An amazing new interpretation of endtime prophecy explains the events in detail.

Who will Escape the Tribulation?

The Lord Jesus described the Great Tribulation with these words: "For then shall be great tribulation, such as was not since the beginning of the world to this time, no, nor ever shall be" (Matthew 24:21).

I would like to emphasize that this is not the same tribulation that the world has experienced since the fall of man. Millions of people experience some type of tribulation in their lives. We are speaking here of an incomparable catastrophe and destruction the world has never seen.

How can we determine that this Great Tribulation is not something that has already happened? Or as some have suggested that we are already in the beginning of it? Let me list six major points which demonstrate that we are not in the time of the Great Tribulation:

- The world is not yet united.
- Mankind is religiously diverse and we have no evidence that Revelation 13:8 is being fulfilled now.
- There is no temple in Jerusalem in which the Antichrist can commit "the overspreading of abomination."
- Our leaders do not yet have "one mind" (Revelation 17:13).
- The Lord has not gathered the nations of the world to the Battle of Armageddon.
- The Church of Jesus Christ is still present on earth.

The Great Tribulation Prophetically

We read of prophecies throughout the Old Testament that describe a terrible day that will come upon the earth. It is called the Day of the Lord. Let us read a few of the verses that describe this day: "Howl ye; for the day of the LORD is at hand; it shall come as a destruction from the Almighty" (Isaiah 13:6).

Fierce Anger: "Behold, the day of the Lord cometh, cruel both with wrath and fierce anger, to lay the land desolate: and he shall destroy the sinners thereof out of it" (Isaiah 13:9).

Vengeance: "For this is the day of the Lord God of hosts, a day of vengeance, that he may avenge him of his adversaries: and the sword shall devour, and it shall be satiate and made drunk with their blood: for the Lord God of hosts hath a sacrifice in the north country by the river Euphrates" (Jeremiah 46:10).

Destruction: "Alas for the day! for the day of the Lord is at hand, and as a destruction from the Almighty shall it come" (Joel 1:15).

The Voice: "The great day of the Lord is near, it is near, and hasteth greatly, even the voice of the day of the Lord: the mighty man shall cry there bitterly" (Zephaniah 1:14).

In reading these few passages, we can sense that this terrible day is not some natural catastrophe or war, not even a world war. Nor is it a form of punishment upon the people on earth. This is the Great

Tribulation, the Day of the Lord, and it is a judgment that leads to destruction. Let me explain.

Salvation vs. Destruction

Children of God repeatedly experience the Lord's chastising hand, not unto destruction but unto salvation. Hebrews 12 explains the purpose of His chastisement: "And ye have forgotten the exhortation which speaketh unto you as unto children, My son, despise not thou the chastening of the Lord, nor faint when thou art rebuked of him: For whom the Lord loveth he chasteneth, and scourgeth every son whom he receiveth. If ye endure chastening, God dealeth with you as with sons; for what son is he whom the father chasteneth not?" (Hebrews 12:5-7).

The Old Testament Scriptures we quoted concerning the Day of the Lord do not deal with God's love but with "destruction," "fierce anger," and "vengeance." Apparently grace will not be present on this Day of the Lord, not because God delights in pronouncing destructive judgment upon people, but because it is the expected execution of God's righteousness upon unrighteousness.

We must remember, "God so loved the world, that He gave His only begotten Son, that whosoever believeth in him should not perish, but have everlasting life" (John 3:16). He has patiently offered this gift for almost 2,000 years but during this time the nations have collectively rejected the only escape from the destructive Tribulation that will come upon earth.

The Wrath of the Lamb

Not only did man refuse God's offer of salvation, but when His wrath comes upon the earth we will see a rebellious reaction from the people:

> And the kings of the earth, and the great men, and the rich men, and the chief captains, and the mighty men, and every bondman, and every free man, hid themselves in the dens and in the rocks of the mountains; And said to the mountains and rocks, Fall on us, and hide us from the face of him that sitteth on the throne, and from the wrath of the Lamb (Revelation 6:15-16).

Interestingly, the religious people will begin to pray, not to Jesus, but to the rocks and the mountains to hide them from wrath of the Lamb. The blood of the Lamb of God will no longer be active for these people. The time of grace will have passed. The One who could have been the salvation of each and every person on earth will now become their Judge!

This is unusual because a lamb is a meek animal that is not aggressive. It follows patiently in the footsteps of the shepherd. Now we see the other side of the Lamb of God. The people who vainly attempt to escape do not see the Lion of the tribe of Judah, but rather the wrath of the Lamb. This is extremely significant. Those who have rejected God's free offer of salvation will be confronted with the Savior, the Lamb of God, who could have saved them but it will be too late.

Refusal to Repent

Later in the book of Revelation we read that repentance will be nonexistent:

> And the rest of the men which were not killed by these plagues yet repented not of the works of their hands, that they should not worship devils, and idols of gold, and silver, and brass, and stone, and of wood: which neither can see, nor hear, nor walk: Neither repented they of their murders, nor of their sorceries, nor of their fornication, nor of their thefts (Revelation 9:20-21).

Mankind will be involved in the manufacturing of his and her own gods to the extent that it will become virtually impossible for them to believe anything else. Here we see 2 Thessalonians 2:11 fulfilled: "And for this cause God shall send them strong delusion, that they should believe a lie."

The Ultimate Blasphemers

As if it were not enough that these people will try to hide from the wrath of the Lamb and refuse to repent, they will blaspheme the very God who has power over destructive punishment. In Revelation 16 we read:

> And men were scorched with great heat, and blasphemed the name of God, which hath power over these plagues: and they repented not to give him glory. And the fifth angel poured out his vial upon the seat of the beast; and his kingdom was full of darkness; and they gnawed their tongues for pain, And blasphemed the God of heaven because of their pains and their sores, and repented not of their deeds (verses 9-11).

The Purpose of the Great Tribulation

We have already determined that the Tribulation is the implementation of God's destructive judgment upon a rebellious humanity. The Tribulation will be the climax of the confrontation between light and darkness, truth and lies, life and death, salvation and damnation; therefore, the purpose for the Tribulation is the destruction of the Gentile democratic world system. But there is another key purpose for the Great Tribulation: the salvation of His people Israel.

Ezekiel and Obadiah both emphasized that the Day of the Lord is directed toward the heathen: "For the day is near, even the day of the LORD is near, a cloudy day; it shall be the time of the heathen" (Ezekiel 30:3). "For the day of the LORD is near upon all the heathen: as thou hast done, it shall be done unto thee: thy reward shall return upon thine own head" (Obadiah 1:15).

Why won't this destructive judgment be directed toward the people of Israel? Because it was only the

Jews who were blinded by God and became enemies of the Gospel for the sake of the Gentiles. Romans 11:28 says, "As concerning the gospel, they are enemies for your sakes: but as touching the election, they are beloved for the fathers sakes."

Gentiles to Comfort Israel

Although the Jews are the enemies of the Gospel, we must remember that it is for our sake; therefore, we must note the Old Testament admonition that is addressed to the Gentiles concerning Israel: "Comfort ye, comfort ye my people, saith your God. Speak ye comfortably to Jerusalem, and cry unto her, that her warfare is accomplished, that her iniquity is pardoned: for she hath received of the LORD'S hand double for all her sins" (Isaiah 40:1-2). God is admonishing the Gentiles to comfort Jerusalem, to speak favorably toward His people who have received a double portion of punishment for sin.

Double Portion of Punishment Prophesied

Obviously, this did not take place during the Babylonian captivity. We read the people's confession in Ezra 9:13: "And after all that is come upon us for our evil deeds, and for our great trespass, seeing that thou our God hast punished us less than our iniquities deserve, and hast given us such deliverance as this." At that time, the Jews had not received a double portion of punishment but less than they deserved! That is their confession!

Isaiah and Jeremiah predicted a double portion of punishment, "For your shame ye shall have double; and for confusion they shall rejoice in their portion: therefore in their land they shall possess the double: everlasting joy shall be unto them" (Isaiah 61:7). "And first I will recompense their iniquity and their sin double; because they have defiled my land, they have filled mine inheritance with the carcases of their detestable and abominable things" (Jeremiah 16:18).

Therefore, we must conclude that from the time of Babylonian captivity to their final return to the land of Israel in the 1900s, the Jews have received a double portion of punishment for their sins.

14 Million Jews Killed

Think about 70 A.D. when the temple was destroyed and a great multitude of Jews were killed by the Romans. What about the Spanish Inquisition and the repeated killing of Jews throughout Europe during the Middle Ages, especially during the papal crusades! And finally, consider the Holocaust, during which over six million Jews were ruthlessly murdered under the leadership of Nazi Germany.

Jewish historians claim that more than 14 million Jews have been murdered since 70 A.D. Thus the question arises, "Have the Gentile nations comforted the Jews and Jerusalem as God commanded?" Not at all! As a matter of fact, the world has never been as united in its opposition of Israel and the land God gave them than it is today.

Gentiles Parting the Holy Land

Joel wrote about another reason for the destructive Tribulation upon the Gentile nations: "I will also gather all nations, and will bring them down into the valley of Jehoshaphat, and will plead with them there for my people and for my heritage Israel, whom they have scattered among the nations, and parted my land" (Joel 3:2). Interestingly enough, the text says all nations; they indeed parted the land that God calls His.

We see the same distinction between these two types of judgments through the Great Tribulation in Isaiah 60:2: "For, behold, the darkness shall cover the earth, and gross darkness the people: but the LORD shall arise upon thee, and his glory shall be seen upon thee."

Jerusalem: The Stumbling Stone

As if that were not enough, the nations are occupied, not only with the land of Israel, but with the city of God, the city of Jerusalem. Here is what Zechariah wrote: "Behold, I will make Jerusalem a cup of trembling unto all the people round about, when they shall be in the siege both against Judah and against Jerusalem. And in that day will I make Jerusalem a burdensome stone for all people: all that burden themselves with it shall be cut in pieces, though all the people of the earth be gathered together against it" (Zechariah 12:2-3).

Now we read the admonition written in Isaiah 40:1-2 in a different light. The Gentile nations do the exact opposite of God's command to comfort the Jews and Jerusalem!

Israel's Hope in Destruction

When the Great Tribulation comes upon earth, specifically for Israel, the Jews will experience such utter devastation, but just when all seems hopeless Israel's unexpected hope will be realized:

> And it shall come to pass in that day, that I will seek to destroy all the nations that come against Jerusalem. And I will pour upon the house of David, and upon the inhabitants of Jerusalem, the spirit of grace and of supplications: and they shall look upon me whom they have pierced, and they shall mourn for him, as one mourneth for his only son, and shall be in bitterness for him, as one that is in bitterness for his first-born (Zechariah 12:9-10).

Therewith, we have established the first group of people who will escape the destructive judgment of the Great Tribulation: the Jews.

Two-Thirds of the World's Population Will Be Killed

The Church, which is the hindering element for the Great Tribulation, will also escape in accordance with

1 Thessalonians 5:9: "For God hath not appointed us to wrath, but to obtain salvation by our Lord Jesus Christ."

The population of the world will be reduced to approximately a third. Many from the remnant of the Gentiles who have survived the apocalyptic catastrophes will enter into the thousand-year kingdom of peace.

We must see one thing clearly: the Millennium will not begin instantaneously for all nations when the Great Tribulation ends, but it will happen over a period of time. Nevertheless, the Great Tribulation will end when the Lord Jesus Christ appears on and rules from the Mount of Olives. Then the remnant of the nations will be categorized and judged according to their works. This event has no relationship to eternal salvation, for we are dealing now with earthly things. The Lord's government will be executed from Jerusalem.

Egypt Will Be Judged

> Therefore thus saith the Lord GOD; Behold, I will bring a sword upon thee, and cut off man and beast out of thee. And the land of Egypt shall be desolate and waste; and they shall know that I am the LORD: because he hath said, The river is mine, and I have made it. Behold, therefore I am against thee, and against thy rivers, and I will make the land of Egypt utterly waste and desolate, from the tower of Syene even unto the border of Ethiopia. No foot of man shall pass through it,

> nor foot of beast shall pass through it, neither shall it be inhabited forty years. And I will make the land of Egypt desolate in the midst of the countries that are desolate, and her cities among the cities that are laid waste shall be desolate forty years: and I will scatter the Egyptians among the nations, and will disperse them through the countries. Yet thus saith the Lord GOD; At the end of forty years will I gather the Egyptians from the people whither they were scattered (Ezekiel 29:8-13).

This judgment has obviously not yet taken place, but it will before Egypt enters into the Millennium of peace.

The Real Escape

You can escape God's wrath right now. You can have absolute assurance that you will be in the presence of the Lord for eternity. The only way to escape is through the person who declared, "I am the way!" Jesus Christ is the truth. He is the light of the world. He is the Son of the living God. When you believe in Him, you have passed "out of darkness into His marvelous light" (1 Peter 2:9).

Read the promise of Romans 8:1, "There is therefore now no condemnation to them which are in Christ Jesus, who walk not after the flesh, but after the Spirit."

How can you belong to this select group? The answer is almost too simple. Come to Jesus, confess your sins and thank Him for pouring out His precious blood for your sins and making you a child of God for all eternity. John 3:36 testifies, "He that believeth on the Son hath everlasting life: and he that believeth not the Son shall not see life; but the wrath of God abideth on him."

That is the only escape! Salvation can only come through Jesus Christ. And when you accept Him as your personal Savior you will belong to the Church of Jesus Christ!

CHAPTER 20

COUNTDOWN TO THE RAPTURE

The end stages of the endtimes have begun. The Great Tribulation is not far off; therefore, we must identify the events that will take place so that the separation between Israel and the Church can occur. The two halves of the Tribulation Period are expounded and the "fallen tabernacle of David" is identified in this chapter.

The Great Tribulation

When will the Great Tribulation begin? In recent years, I have read several articles written by people who argue that the Great Tribulation is not seven years but only 3 1/2.

To establish a rebuttal to this claim, we must first answer this question: What makes the Great Tribulation recognizable? For one thing, darkness shall cover the earth as we read in Isaiah 60:2. Why will it be dark? Because the light of the Church has been removed from the earth. Jesus said, "Ye are the light of the world" (Matthew 5:14). Christians are the light of the world because we are united with Jesus, who said, "I am the light of the world: he that followeth me shall not walk in darkness, but shall have the light of life" (John 8:12). Therefore, to answer the question regarding the duration of the Great Tribulation, we must take a closer look at the hindering element: the Church.

Rapture: The Beginning of the Countdown

The Church will be removed from the earth in an event known as the Rapture. The Bible states that the Rapture will occur at a time "when ye think not" (Luke 12:40). The Lord will come suddenly and without warning; therefore, we cannot identify the time when the Great Tribulation will begin because we cannot predict the time of the Rapture.

We do know, however, that darkness will spread

across the face of the earth when the Church is removed from this world. When that takes place Satan will have a field day. The people left behind will do as they please because the light will no longer be around to expose their wickedness. Everything that is of God will then be done away with. Daniel described the Antichrist as "a king of fierce countenance, and understanding dark sentences" who will fulfill his intentions because the Church is no longer here.

What is the Rapture?

The word Rapture is not found in any of the major English translations of the Bible. While much has been written on this subject and many theologians are beginning to oppose the reality of the Rapture, let us read two verses that distinctly teach the Church's removal from the earth: "For the Lord himself shall descend from heaven with a shout, with the voice of the archangel, and with the trump of God: and the dead in Christ shall rise first: Then we which are alive and remain shall be caught up together with them in the clouds, to meet the Lord in the air: and so shall we ever be with the Lord" (1 Thessalonians 4:16-17).

There is no indication in Scripture that reveals the time of our departure, but the Bible simply concludes, "Wherefore comfort one another with these words" (verse 18). Paul is obviously referring here to the preceding verses that explain the Rapture and now states that waiting for this event will be our comfort.

There is no doubt that numerous Christians who lived with persecution and faced severe punishment and even death did indeed hold fast to the comfort that Jesus could return at any moment.

The Church and Israel

Before we continue, we must point out that there is a clear distinction between the Church of Jesus Christ and the nation of Israel. If Israel is God's chosen people and they are alive during the Tribulation Period, then why wouldn't they be considered a light to the world? Let's look at the Word of God for an answer. Acts 15 contains an amazing prophecy. The purpose of this first apostolic council was to discuss the membership of the Gentiles in the Church because there was some confusion about the distinction between the Jews and Gentiles.

We quickly learn that this type of church business meeting was much like the ones we experience today. In verse 7 we read that a disagreement had taken place within the Church: "And when there had been much disputing." Finally, however, we read in verses 13-14: "After they had held their peace, James answered, saying, Men and brethren, hearken unto me: Simeon hath declared how God at the first did visit the Gentiles, to take out of them a people for his name." James repeated Peter's message and added, "And to this agree the words of the prophets; as it is written" (verse 15). Here, a determination based on the Bible is being made that agrees with the prophets. They surely believed the written Word of God!

Separation by the Tabernacle

Now comes the revelation of the distinction between Israel and the Church, "After this I will return, and will build again the tabernacle of David, which is fallen down; and I will build again the ruins thereof, and I will set it up" (verse 16). In verse 14, God has taken out a people for His Name from among the Gentiles — the Church. And in verse 16, He is returning to Israel to rebuild her.

Our heavenly Father has been taking out a people from among the Gentiles for His name's sake for almost 2,000 years. I believe that His selection is almost complete because Israel's reemergence has become a modern reality. I believe we can expect the last one from among the Gentiles to be added to the Church and therewith, the number will be complete; that is, the last one from among the Gentiles will have been added to the Church and the Rapture will take place!

The Fallen Tabernacle of David

Has God already begun to resurrect the fallen tabernacle of David? To answer this question, we must first ask, "What is this fallen tabernacle of David?" James was quoting Amos 9:11, which reads,

"In that day will I raise up the tabernacle of David that is fallen, and close up the breaches thereof; and I will raise up his ruins, and I will build it as in the days of old."

This tabernacle must not be confused with the tabernacle/tent David had pitched to house the Ark of the Covenant: "And they brought in the ark of the LORD, and set it in his place, in the midst of the tabernacle that David had pitched for it: and David offered burnt offerings and peace offerings before the LORD" (2 Samuel 6:17).

Acts 15:16 reads: "And I will build again the ruins thereof." Ruins generally refer to stones that were thrown about, broken down and in need of reassembly, but because there never was a tabernacle of David made from stones, we know that Acts 15:16 does not refer to a literal tent-like tabernacle. Thus, this fallen tabernacle actually represents Israel's national identity!

More than One Tabernacle?

How do we know for sure that Acts 15:16 is not referring to the literal tabernacle? Let's look at an example. It was argued during David's time over which tribe should be the leader of the tribes of Israel. Some people probably thought Joseph should have been put in a position of leadership since he was responsible for saving his brothers and establishing the nation of Israel in Egypt but the Bible clearly states, "Moreover he [God] refused the tabernacle of Joseph, and chose not the tribe of Ephraim" (Psalm 78:67). Here we see that the word "tabernacle" does not exclusively refer to the tabernacle of the Ark of the Covenant.

Furthermore we read in Amos 9:12: "That they [Israel] may possess the remnant of Edom, and of all the heathen, which are called by my name, saith the Lord that doeth this." Here He identifies the relationship between Israel and the Church: "and of all the heathen, which are called by my name."

The Church and Israel are Organically One

Although Israel and the Church are different identities, they are organically united: Romans 11 makes this very clear. As Gentiles, we are contrary to nature, grafted into the natural olive tree, which is Israel: "For if thou wert cut out of the olive tree which is wild by nature, and wert graffed contrary to nature into a good olive tree: how much more shall these, which be the natural branches, be graffed into their own olive tree?" (Romans 11:24). Thus, Christians from among the Gentiles are one with Israel. The Church and Israel have the same roots.

To summarize: the resurrection of David's fallen tabernacle is the return of the Jewish people to their land in our day. Realizing that these things are happening now, we can only conclude that the time of the Church is reaching an end. Not only is the Church of

Jesus Christ connected with Israel, but Israel's salvation is connected to the fullness of the Gentiles. In his letter to the Romans, Paul wrote, "blindness in part is happened to Israel, until the fulness of the Gentiles be come in. And so all Israel shall be saved" (Romans 11:25-26).

Seven Years of Great Tribulation

The fact that Israel is increasing in stature today is an additional sign for the Church that the time of the Rapture is at hand and we are drawing closer to the beginning of the Great Tribulation.

According to my understanding of the prophetic Word, the day Israel gains acceptance into the European Union, which we have identified as the resurrected Roman Empire, and becomes part of the world family of nations, they will have ignored God's command for them to be a peculiar people — that will be the beginning of the Antichrist covenant.

Daniel described a covenant that will initiate the beginning of the Great Tribulation: "And he shall confirm the covenant with many for one week: and in the midst of the week he shall cause the sacrifice and the oblation to cease, and for the overspreading of abominations he shall make it desolate, even until the consummation, and that determined shall be poured upon the desolate" (Daniel 9:27).

Here we have a time span that is clearly associated with the Great Tribulation: one week. According to

Daniel 9:24-26, we know that this "week" means seven years — each day of this week represents one year. How do we know this? In verse 24 the angel Gabriel tells Daniel, "Seventy weeks are determined upon thy people and upon thy holy city, to finish the transgression, and to make an end of sins, and to make reconciliation for iniquity, and to bring in everlasting righteousness." Seventy times seven equals 490. A period of 483 years begins with the commandment to restore Jerusalem and ends with the act of reconciliation through the Lord Jesus Christ on Calvary's cross. That leaves seven years for the Tribulation Period, which ends in the arrival of everlasting righteousness!

What happened to the 2,000 years in between? Daniel wrote about the crucifixion in his prophetic timetable, "After three score and two weeks shall Messiah be cut off, but not for himself." Martin Luther translated this verse as, "After sixty-two weeks, the anointed shall be destroyed and nothing shall be." And the Tanakh reads: "After those sixty-two weeks, the anointed will disappear and vanish." In the margin of the Tanakh is written, "Meaning in Hebrew uncertain," regarding the verse, "the Anointed will disappear" but the meaning is very clear. The anointed shall be in the presence of the Father for about 2,000 years, absent from Israel — vanished!

The Tribulation: Part Two

It is important to realize that the Bible focuses primarily on the second half of the Great Tribulation. The first 3 1/2 years will be glorious. Men will pride themselves on their achievement of peace and prosperity. Conflicts will be quickly resolved. How do we know this? There is little, if any, chance for opposition under the Antichrist because the Bible says, "Who is able to make war with him?" (Revelation 13:4).

False Peace

The people will remember all of the acts of unrighteousness that were committed for thousands of years, but they will believe that it has finally reached an end. Politicians will echo Great Britain's Neville Chamberlain as he exited a meeting with Hitler, "Peace in our time!" The conflict between the nations, states and races of people will be solved. Religious leaders will extol their systems for bringing peace to the world. There will be no difference between Catholics and Protestants, Jews and Muslims, Hindus or Buddhists. They will all become one, rejoicing in peace, and giving honor and glory to their gods. All religions will be brought together under one roof. The people will decide that there is but one god (although they will pick a false one) who may be worshiped by different names. Here we need to explain that the various religions will not deny their identity. In other words, a Muslim will remain a Muslim and so on down the line, but they will nevertheless unite under the motto, "Unity in Diversity." The old Roman slogan, "United We Stand" will be changed to "In Diversity We Stand United." Thus the possibility is open for all religions to come in on equal ground, and such will also be the case politically, economically, and militarily.

New Religion

If such a future is difficult for you to comprehend, especially in light of all the religious conflict we see today, then you should read the following release from 1974:

> Buddhists, Christians, Confucianists, Hindus, Jains, Jews, Muslims, Shintoists, Sikhs, Zoroastrians and still others, we have sought here to listen to the spirit within our varied and venerable religious traditions... We have grappled with the towering issues that our societies must resolve in order to bring about peace, justice, and an ennobling quality of life for every person, and every people... We rejoice that... the long era of prideful, and even prejudiced isolation of the religions of humanity is, we hope, gone forever. We appeal to the religious communities of the world to inculcate the attitude of planetary citizenship.[41]

The Pride of Antichrist

Opposition will not be tolerated in such a New World Order because of the Antichrist's amazing success. His prosperity is again emphasized in Daniel 11:36: "The king shall do according to his will; and he shall exalt himself, and magnify himself above every god, and shall speak marvellous things against the God of gods, and shall prosper till the indignation be accomplished: for that that is determined shall be done." But his pride will spark the beginning of his demise. The Antichrist will declare he is God after 3 1/2 years of unprecedented success. Second Thessalonians 2:4 confirms him as the one, "Who opposeth and exalteth himself above all that is called God, or that is worshipped; so that he as God sitteth in the temple of God, shewing himself that he is God."

Then the second half of the Great Tribulation will begin. How do we know this? The book of Daniel provides the answer, "And he [Antichrist] shall confirm the covenant with many for one week and in the midst of the week: he shall cause the sacrifice and oblation to cease" (Daniel 9:27). Since a "week" means seven years, the "midst" of it is 3 1/2 years. At that time, Israel will recognize that the Antichrist is not the promised Messiah. He will declare himself to be God, but the Jews know that a man cannot be God. Israel, however, is not the one that breaks the covenant — the Antichrist will: "He hath put forth his hands against such as be at peace with him: he hath broken his covenant" (Psalm 55:20).

The End of the Great Tribulation

The second half of the Great Tribulation is also marked by the Antichrist's hatred for the God of heaven, "And he shall speak great words against the most High, and shall wear out the saints of the most High, and think to change times and laws: and they shall be given into his hand until a time and times and the dividing of time" (Daniel 7:25). We see that a very definite time limit is set: "a time and times and the dividing of time." In other words, one year plus two years and six months makes 3 1/2 years!

The beginning of the second half of the Tribulation is marked by the end of the sacrificial system in the rebuilt temple in Jerusalem and the proclamation of the Antichrist to be God, which leads to his request to be worshiped: "Yea, he magnified himself even to the prince of the host, and by him the daily sacrifice was taken away, and the place of the sanctuary was cast down. And an host was given him against the daily sacrifice by reason of transgression, and it cast down the truth to the ground; and it practised, and prospered" (Daniel 8:11-12). He continues to prosper even throughout the last half of the Great Tribulation.

Now no one will be able to stop him. He will hold the power in his hand and consider himself to be God: "Even him, whose coming is after the working of Satan with all power and signs and lying wonders, And with all deceivableness of unrighteousness in them that perish; because they received not the love of the truth, that they might be saved" (2 Thessalonians 2:9-10).

For all practical purposes, the Antichrist will become the supreme ruler of the world. Only Israel will oppose him and as a result the Jewish people will be persecuted so severely that God will have to intervene supernaturally in order to protect His people: "And to the woman were given two wings of a great eagle, that she might fly into the wilderness, into her place, where she is nourished for a time, and times, and half a time, from the face of the serpent" (Revelation 12:14).

Again we read, "a time, and times, and half a time," meaning 3 1/2 years. When these 3 1/2 years are over, the Lord will put an end to the powers of darkness with His appearance, which is recorded in 2 Thessalonians 2:8, "And then shall that Wicked be revealed, whom the Lord shall consume with the spirit of his mouth, and shall destroy with the brightness of his coming." That will be the end of the Great Tribulation!

Climax of Deception

We can barely imagine the deception that will commence when Satan and his angels are cast out of heaven to earth. He will roam this planet because the light of the world, which dwells in the Church will be gone.

In addition, the bottomless pit will be opened and more devils will come out to torment mankind: "And he opened the bottomless pit; and there arose a smoke out of the pit, as the smoke of a great furnace; and the sun and the air were darkened by reason of the smoke of the pit. And there came out of the smoke locusts upon the earth: and unto them was given power, as the scorpions of the earth have power" (Revelation 9:2-3). These "locusts" are part of the underworld coming out of the bottomless pit as members of Satan's army; therefore, we can understand why Jesus and the prophets spoke of this time as being the most terrible time on earth. Revelation 12:12 reveals the contrast: "Therefore rejoice, ye heavens, and ye that dwell in them. Woe to the inhabiters of the earth and of the sea! for the devil is come down unto you, having great wrath, because he knoweth that he hath but a short time."

The Name or the Number of the Beast

If life on earth is impossible, seeing that those who refuse to worship the image will be killed and existence is out of the question without the Mark of the Beast or the number of his name, who will remain but the remnant of Israel? Scripture makes it clear that nations will exist after the Great Tribulation and the Gentiles will come and worship in Jerusalem.

It is also evident that our Lord will rule the nations from Jerusalem with a rod of iron: "And she brought forth a man child, who was to rule all nations with a rod of iron: and her child was caught up unto God, and to his throne" (Revelation 12:5). How can this prophecy be fulfilled if there aren't any nations left?

What about Moses' prophecy? "For the LORD thy God blesseth thee, as he promised thee: and thou shalt lend unto many nations, but thou shalt not borrow; and thou shalt reign over many nations, but they shall not reign over thee" (Deuteronomy 15:6). How will Israel rule if there aren't any nations left?

The Mark of the Beast

I propose that we take another look at Revelation 13:15-17:

> And he had power to give life unto the image of the beast, that the image of the beast should both speak, and cause that as many as would not worship the image of the beast should be killed. And he causeth all, both small and great, rich and poor, free and bond, to receive a mark in their right hand, or in their foreheads: And that no man might buy or sell, save he that had the mark, or the name of the beast, or the number of his name.

Death is not caused by the Antichrist or the false prophet but by the image of the beast. The image executes the death sentence upon a non-worshiper, "that the image of the beast should both speak and cause that as many as would not worship the image of the beast should be killed" (Revelation 13:15).

Verse 16 makes it clear that there will be no exceptions: All people on earth will be required to receive a mark in their right hand or in their foreheads.

Dr. Wim Malgo interpreted this as those who receive the mark in their right hand will be the manual laborers, and those who receive it in their foreheads will be the intellectuals. Verse 17 clearly explains that it will be impossible for anyone to survive, "save he that had the mark, or the name of the beast, or the number of his name."

Two Different Marks

After searching through many translations, I have come to the conclusion that the Mark of the Beast consists of two categories. From the best sources I have studied, it should read, "save he that had the mark, which is the name of the beast or the number of his name." Therefore, we should deal with two categories: 1) those who receive the Mark of the Beast and 2) those who receive the number of his name.

We must now determine what will happen to these two categories of people. What does the Bible say? When we read the book of Revelation we notice that the Mark of the Beast is mentioned five times. Three times it talks of eternal punishment and two times about the victory over the Mark of the Beast.

- "And the smoke of their torment ascendeth up for ever and ever: and they have no rest day nor night, who worship the beast and his image, and whosoever receiveth the mark of his name" (Revelation 14:11). This means eternal punishment "for ever and ever" for those who worship the image of the beast and those who receive the mark of his name.

• "And the first went, and poured out his vial upon the earth; and there fell a noisome and grievous sore upon the men which had the mark of the beast, and upon them which worshipped his image" (Revelation 16:2). Again, torment for those who have taken the Mark of the Beast and have worshiped his image.

• "And the beast was taken, and with him the false prophet that wrought miracles before him, with which he deceived them that had received the mark of the beast, and them that worshipped his image. These both were cast alive into a lake of fire burning with brimstone" (Revelation 19:20). Once more, we see the image worshiper who received the Mark of the Beast.

• "And I saw as it were a sea of glass mingled with fire: and them that had gotten the victory over the beast, and over his image, and over his mark, and over the number of his name, stand on the sea of glass, having the harps of God" (Revelation 15:2). Their victory is: 1) over the beast, 2) over the image, 3) over his mark, and 4) over the number of his name. Here we see a very special group of believers who will come out of the Great Tribulation.

• "And I saw thrones, and they sat upon them, and judgment was given unto them: and I saw the souls of them that were beheaded for the witness of Jesus, and for the word of God, and which had not worshipped the beast, neither his image, neither had received his mark upon their foreheads, or in their hands; and they lived and reigned with Christ a thousand years" (Revelation 20:4).

What we learn from these five verses is that those who are condemned forever have received 1) the Mark of the Beast and 2) have worshiped the image. We do not read, however, that those who have accepted the number of his name are in the same category as the condemned. Nevertheless, they will not belong to the ones who sing in victory the song of Moses and the song of the Lamb (Revelation 15:3). Therefore, I propose that the ones who receive the number of his name will enter the Millennial Kingdom of peace. That fact, however, does not mean they are saved. Jesus will rule with a rod of iron and sinners will die for their sins during the Millennium. The assumption that only the saved will enter the Millennium is incorrect.

It is my understanding from Scripture that a great multitude will not worship the image, nor will they receive the Mark of the Beast, but they will take the number of his name in order to survive, which means they are still sinners in need of redemption.

In his unregenerate state, man is corrupt to the core, but sin will no longer be tolerated during the Millennial Reign of Christ. It is quite obvious that those who enter the kingdom will still be capable of committing sin. Thus, we read in Isaiah 65:20: "There shall be no more thence an infant of days, nor an old man that hath not filled his days: for the child shall die an hundred years old; but the sinner being an hundred years old shall be accursed." The last sentence in the Tanakh reads: "And he who fails to reach a hundred shall be reckoned accursed." Again, entering the Millennium does not mean a person is saved. Sinners will die and "shall be accursed," but there will be no more sinners on earth when the thousand years are over — only saints will remain!

I am fully aware that this interpretation is new, but I felt impressed to present it to the Church and let you judge based on the Word of God. According to my understanding of Scripture, this is the only way to have literal nations live on earth besides the Jews in the Millennium.

CHAPTER 21

THE MILLENNIUM: BEGINNING AND END

The Lord Jesus Christ will put an end to Satan's kingdom and power. This chapter reveals Satan's origin and his ultimate destination. We also provide a revealing interpretation of Revelation's Gog and Magog and the Mark of the Beast.

Who Shall Populate the Millennium?

We read about the thousand-year kingdom of peace in Revelation 20:1-7.

First, we will emphasize four important subjects:

- The arrest, conviction, and sentencing of the deceiver, the hindering element for genuine peace.
- Believers who come out of the Great Tribulation and rule with Christ for a thousand years.
- The first resurrection and the abolition of the second death for those who are part of the first resurrection.
- Satan's temporary release and final end.

> And I saw an angel come down from heaven, having the key of the bottomless pit and a great chain in his hand. And he laid hold on the dragon, that old serpent, which is the Devil, and Satan, and bound him a thousand years, And cast him into the bottomless pit, and shut him up, and set a seal upon him, that he should deceive the nations no more, till the thousand years should be fulfilled: and after that he must be loosed a little season. And I saw thrones, and they sat upon them, and judgment was given unto them: and I saw the souls of them that were beheaded for the witness of Jesus, and for the word of God, and which had not worshipped the beast, neither his image, neither had received his mark upon their foreheads, or in their hands; and they lived and reigned with Christ a thousand years. But the rest of the dead lived not again until the thousand years were finished. This is the first resurrection. Blessed and holy is he that hath part in the first

> resurrection: on such the second death hath no power, but they shall be priests of God and of Christ, and shall reign with him a thousand years. And when the thousand years are expired, Satan shall be loosed out of his prison (Revelation 20:1-7).

Satan's Arrest

In the above Scripture, we read that the angel who comes down from heaven is not confronting the dragon. There is no battle, nor is there any resistance. This is strictly the arrest of Satan, also known as the dragon, the old serpent, the devil. We read, "And he [the angel] laid hold on the dragon." Satan is securely bound and cast into the bottomless pit whereupon a seal is set so that he cannot escape and deceive the nations.

Why didn't Satan resist his arrest? After all, he is the great rebellious one. We could imagine that his refusal to cooperate would cause quite a problem. The fact that he had to be taken and laid hold on reveals that he will be powerless, but that he had to be bound indicates that this is not the final judgment and that the devil remains a potential threat.

The reason the angel does not need to fight is based on the fact that Satan is already a defeated foe. His lying and deceptive nature will be exposed at the appearance of the Lord, and therewith, he will be stripped of his power in the presence of the Omnipotent One.

The Apostle Paul describes this event in just one verse: "And then shall that Wicked be revealed, whom the Lord shall consume with the spirit of his mouth, and shall destroy with the brightness of his coming" (2 Thessalonians 2:8). Note that the Lord will not defeat Satan with His power but He will destroy him with "the brightness of His coming."

Jesus is the light of the world. There is no darkness wherever the Lord is — nothing can be hidden. He has eyes like "a flame of fire" (Revelation 1:14).

John testified that Jesus is the light of men: "In him was life; and the life was the light of men" (John 1:4). This light was rejected because of Satan's deceptive activity to keep men in darkness. Thus, we read in verse 5: "And the light shineth in darkness; and the darkness comprehended it not."

No More Deception

Satan's arrest has another specific purpose: God stops Satan from deceiving the nations any longer. It is significant that the time of Satan's imprisonment is documented as being a thousand years.

We know from Scripture that one day is with the Lord as a thousand years, and a thousand years as one day. No man has ever lived for a thousand years because God said, "for in the day that thou eatest thereof thou shalt surely die" (Genesis 2:17). Adam, to whom this warning was addressed, lived 933 years!

During the Great Tribulation

Peace will begin after Satan has been arrested and incapacitated. We read that a special category of believers will rule with Jesus for a thousand years. This is a specific group of believers who are identified as those who:

- Were beheaded for the witness of Jesus and for the Word of God
- Have not worshiped the beast
- Nor his image
- Nor have they received the mark upon their forehead or on their hand

These people will live and reign with Christ for a thousand years! Obviously, there must be other people on earth at that time over which these saints will rule with the Lord.

Where is the Church?

Scripture makes it clear that the Church, which is the Body of Christ, will be raptured from the earth before the Tribulation begins. We will remain in His presence from that moment forward. Our actual position is described in 1 Thessalonians 4:17: "and so shall we ever be with the Lord." Therefore, wherever the Lord is, there we shall be also. When He returns to earth and rules we too will be a part of it because we are His Body. The Bible does not identify our function as the Body of Christ while we are with the Lord on earth other than the fact that we too shall rule with a rod of iron.

The First Resurrection

Jesus is the first fruit from among the dead: He is the beginning of the first resurrection. The Rapture of the Church is the finalization of His resurrection. It is a demonstration of His absolute victory over death, as it is written: "then shall be brought to pass the saying that is written, Death is swallowed up in victory. O death, where is thy sting? O grave, where is thy victory?" (1 Corinthians 15:54-55). Prophetically speaking, however, the first resurrection continues, just as salvation in Jesus Christ will continue after the Rapture.

Why is Satan Temporarily Paroled?

According to Habakkuk 2:14 the world will be filled with the knowledge of the Lord during the reign of Christ on earth: "For the earth shall be filled with the knowledge of the glory of the LORD, as the waters cover the sea." The deceiver will be incapacitated and people will no longer be led astray. Thus, the logical question we need to ask is why God allows Satan's release from his prison after the thousand years is over?

The result of his release is described in Revelation 20: 8-9: "And shall go out to deceive the nations which are in the four quarters of the earth, Gog, and Magog, to gather them together to battle: the number of whom is as the sand of the sea. And they went up on the breadth of the earth, and compassed the camp of the saints about, and the beloved city: and fire came down from God out of heaven, and devoured them."

Scripture seems to indicate that Satan will use his deceptive capabilities to gather the nations, who then will arm themselves in order to make war against the beloved city.

We cannot fully recognize the events that will take place in the future, but it is my understanding that the nations mentioned in verse 8 are the fallen angels who originally sided with Satan and not literal nations of human beings. I am fully aware that most, if not all, scholars of eschatology view the event described in Revelation 20 differently, but I have found it necessary to reanalyze various interpretations, and what I present here is not the ultimate interpretation. It does, however, seem like a logical answer.

Satan's Beginning

Let's read Isaiah's account of Satan's origin and end:

> How art thou fallen from heaven, O Lucifer, son of the morning! how art thou cut down to the ground, which didst weaken the nations! For thou hast said in thine heart, I will ascend into heaven, I will exalt my throne above the stars of

> God: I will sit also upon the mount of the congregation, in the sides of the north: I will ascend above the heights of the clouds; I will be like the most High. Yet thou shalt be brought down to hell, to the sides of the pit (Isaiah 14:12-15).

We must remember that this statement is a prophecy of Satan's origin and his end. The fallen nations, which are the fallen angels, are already in hell. They are powerless and they see Satan coming and ask, "Are thou also become weak as we? Are thou become like unto us?" (verse 10). Then in verse 12 they identify his position in relationship to the fallen angels, "How art thou cut down to the ground, which didst weaken the nations!" (verse 12). Who are these nations? Apparently they are the nations of fallen angels! Satan did not weaken the nations of people on earth; he is the god of the nations! He strengthens the nations, "Let the weak say I am strong" (Joel 3:10).

We read about the angels who followed Satan in Jude 6: "And the angels which kept not their first estate, but left their own habitation, he hath reserved in everlasting chains under darkness unto the judgment of the great day."

The Stars of Heaven

Let's also take a closer look at the stars. Revelation 12:4 reveals that a third of the stars of heaven were cast upon the earth. This corresponds with Daniel

8:10, where he wrote about the Antichrist: "And it waxed great, even to the host of heaven; and it cast down some of the host and of the stars to the ground, and stamped upon them."

What kind of stars is being referred to here? Take a look at the origin of Satan. Isaiah 14:12 reads, "O Lucifer, son of the morning." Martin Luther translates this verse as, "Thou beautiful star of the morning." The Tanakh says, "O shining One, Son of Dawn." This clearly indicates that Satan was once a glorious creation called the "star of the morning." Only the King James translation attaches the name Lucifer to the star.

When Lucifer fell he took with him one-third of the heavenly angelic hosts. It is evident that these "stars" are not the stars we see in the night sky. Some of the stars we see are significantly larger in size than earth, thus the stars in which the Bible is referring to are fallen angels.

Furthermore, Peter confirms that God cast down the rebellious angels and reserved punishment for them: "For if God spared not the angels that sinned, but cast them down to hell, and delivered them into chains of darkness, to be reserved unto judgment" (2 Peter 2:4).

Enduring Peace

The thousand-year kingdom of peace begins with mankind beating their swords into plowshares. The

Bible reveals that men will learn war no more. The manufacture of weapons will stop. How then can men gather to battle? Isaiah 2:4 testifies, "And he shall judge among the nations, and shall rebuke many people: and they shall beat their swords into plowshares, and their spears into pruninghooks: nation shall not lift up sword against nation, neither shall they learn war any more." We emphasize here the word "anymore."

But there is another reason: the guarantee of peace is subject to the universe: "They [all people] shall fear thee [God] as long as the sun and moon endure, throughout all generations. He shall come down like rain upon the mown grass: as showers that water the earth. In his days shall the righteous flourish: and abundance of peace so long as the moon endureth" (Psalm 72:5-7). Only when the sun and moon have been done away with will this peace cease to exist!

The end of this last battle, the confrontation between the saints and Satan, is described only briefly, "and fire came down from God out of heaven and devoured them." No description of weapons, bodies, or machinery is offered thus we are given here an additional method with which to identify these nations.

Who are Gog and Magog?

What about the names Gog and Magog in Revelation 20:8? Bible scholars agree that Gog and

Magog of Ezekiel 38-39 is an area north of Israel known today as Russia. What was unique about Russia was its attempt to dominate the world through communism. They were not anti-Christian. Communism did not create a religion comparable to Christianity in order to deceive the nations, but they were outspoken and boldly anti-God!

Russian communism found its expression in the rejection of all religion. For more than 70 years the communists lifted up their fists against heaven and shouted, "There is no God!" and "God is dead!" But world communism, which is anti-God, has already received the first part of God's judgment: the disintegration of the Soviet Union. In other words, God said "Communism is dead!"

It is also evident from Ezekiel 38:9,12 that this northern confederacy will invade the land of Israel for gain: "Thou shalt ascend and come like a storm, thou shalt be like a cloud to cover the land, thou, and all thy bands, and many people with thee...To take a spoil, and to take a prey; to turn thine hand upon the desolate places that are now inhabited, and upon the people that are gathered out of the nations, which have gotten cattle and goods, that dwell in the midst of the land."

We read an additional confirmation that the northern confederacy is motivated by material. This is evidenced by the three questions Israel's Arab neighbors ask in protest of the attack: "Sheba, and Dedan, and the merchants of Tarshish, with all the young lions thereof, shall say unto thee, Art thou come to take a spoil? hast thou gathered thy company to take a prey? to carry away silver and gold, to take away cattle and goods, to take a great spoil?" (Ezekiel 38:13). This invasion is aimed at taking goods.

Who Are Sheba, Dedan, and Tarshish?

Sheba was the son of Ramah, a son of Cush, who had settled somewhere on the shores of the Persian Gulf. The Bible also mentions the kingdom of Sheba, which is located in today's Yemen. Dedan is identified as the son of Ramah, the son of Cush (Genesis 10:7, 1 Chronicles 1:9). Dedan is also the son of Jokshan, Abraham's son who he had with Keturah (Genesis 25:3, 1 Chronicles 1:32). *Ungers Bible Dictionary* places the descendants on the Syrian borders near the territory of Edom, located in today's Jordan. While Tarshish cannot be identified geographically, it is mentioned several times in the Old Testament in connection with ships, merchants, and trade from the Mediterranean Sea to the Persian Gulf.

It seems almost natural that the rich Arab states ask some very common, yet frightening questions regarding the true intention of the northern confederacy.

This should suffice to show that the Gog and Magog of Ezekiel 38 and 39 concern a geographically identifiable area, including a group of allied kings designated by name.

Demonic Origin of Gog and Magog

When we read about Gog and Magog in Revelation 20:8, we understand this to be a tangible description of the anti-God sentiment. This should show that the Gog and Magog of Revelation 20 are only related to the Gog and Magog of Ezekiel 38 and 39 because they symbolize the anti-God sentiment. Still, someone may insist that this speaks of the same Gog and Magog.

To explain this further, let's look at some examples, such as the casting down of Satan. Ezekiel compares Lucifer, the former morning star with the king of Tyrus, "Son of man, take up a lamentation upon the king of Tyrus, and say unto him, Thus saith the Lord God" (Ezekiel 28:12). The prophet describes Satan's fall through the judgment pronounced on the king of Tyrus. It is obvious that the king of Tyrus was never in "Eden the garden of God" (Ezekiel 28:13), he never was "the anointed cherub" (Ezekiel 28:14) and he never "walked on the holy mountain of God," or "in the midst of the stones of fire" (verse 14). When Ezekiel described Satan's fall, he used only the king of Tyrus as an example.

Later in history, when our Lord Jesus said to Peter "Get thee behind me, Satan" (Mark 8:33) we know that He was addressing Peter but through him Jesus meant Satan. Remember, Peter had questioned Jesus' prophecy that He would be killed, thus, Satan was using Peter as his mouthpiece.

The Gog and Magog of Revelation 20 is a description of the final rebellion against the living God and has no relationship to the battle of Gog and Magog recorded in Ezekiel 38 and 39. This is the final act of the spirit of "Gog and Magog": rebellion against God!

Satan's End

The casting out of Satan will take place in three phases:

1) At the Rapture, Satan and his angels will be cast out of heaven: "And there was war in heaven: Michael and his angels fought against the dragon; and the dragon fought and his angels, And prevailed not; neither was their place found any more in heaven. And the great dragon was cast out, that old serpent, called the Devil, and Satan, which deceiveth the whole world: he was cast out into the earth, and his angels were cast out with him" (Revelation 12:7-9). This is banishment from heaven: he will never again have access to heaven and accuse the brethren before God.

2) Satan will be arrested and imprisoned at the end of the Great Tribulation. This is banishment from earth; he will no longer be able to deceive the nations.

3) At the end of the thousand-year kingdom of peace he will be loosed for a short time, which God uses to finalize Satan's eternal destiny. This results in

the banishment of Satan's access to the saints and the holy city forever and ever. That is eternity. His final place is described in Revelation 20:10: "And the devil that deceived them was cast into the lake of fire and brimstone, where the beast and the false prophet [are], and shall be tormented day and night for ever and ever."

CONCLUSION

There is no salvation outside of Jesus Christ. Jesus was the only One who could satisfy God's wrath against sinners with the shedding of His blood. We can be saved in His name alone. My primary emphasis throughout this book was that our hope lies in trusting Him, not in manmade religion or democracy. I believe I have thoroughly exposed the danger of trusting in democracy.

Most people would have quickly agreed if I had presented the premise that communism would lead to the establishment of the Antichrist. The same holds true for dictatorship, or any other form of government that restricts our freedom and rules over us without our vote. In our minds, however, democracy equals freedom, and we love and trust it. How ironic it is that what we love, trust and desire as human beings is the exact catalyst that will place God and man on a collision course to final judgment.

Dear reader, the Bible says, "Now is the accepted time; behold, now is the day of salvation" (2

Corinthians 6:2). If you are not a child of God today, confess your sins and acknowledge that you are unable to save yourself. Ask Jesus to come into your heart and thank Him that He has promised in His Word, "And it shall come to pass, that whosoever shall call on the name of the Lord shall be saved" (Acts 2:21).

Eternal bliss awaits those who are saved, and eternal damnation is reserved for those who are lost. You must make a decision. Where will you spend eternity?

ENDNOTES

Chapter 2
1 *The State*, 12/25/94, p.D-1

Chapter 3
2 *The Scotsman,* 1/3/94
3 *U.S.News*, 11/8/93
4 *Jerusalem Post* Intl. Edition, 6/17/95, p.4

Chapter 4
5 *Jerusalem Post*, 1/28/95, p.4
6 *Outpost*, April 1994, p.5
7 *Outpost*, April 1994, p.5
8 *Jerusalem Post,* 1/28/95, p.3
9 *Dispatch From Jerusalem,* 12/93, p.8

Chapter 6
10 *U.S.News* 12/20/93 (Cover story)
11 *The Scotsman,* 5/28/94

Chapter 7
12 *Newsweek,* 5/30/94, p.68
13 *The News and Observer,* 2/9/95

Chapter 8
14 *The State*, 3/19/94, p.D8
15 *Global Peace and the Rise of Antichrist,* Dave Hunt p.129
16 *Far Eastern Economic Rev*iews 2/2/95, p.52

Chapter 9
17 *Wire reports,* 11/26/93
18 *Popular Science*, 1/94
19 *Daily Mail,* 4/2/94
20 *Reuters,* 12/29/93
21 *Christians and Israel,* V.3/No.1, p.5

22 *Kansas City Star,* 1/15/95
23 *The Herald,* 4/4/94

Chapter 10
24 *The State,* 12/12/94
25 *The European,* 3/9/95
26 *Courier Journal,* 5/11/84, p.A7
27 *The Voice, Diocese of Newark,* 1/89
28 *L'Observatore Romano*, 2/10/86, p.5
29 *The European,* 12/15/94, p.1
30 *The European,* 5/26/94, p.25
31 *The State,* 12/3/93

Chapter 11
32 *The State*, 7/6/95, p.B10

Chapter 12
33 *The European*, 7/6/95, p.17

Chapter 13
34 *Know the Marks of Cults*, Dave Breese

Chapter 15
35 *Kansas City Star,* 4/26/92
36 Feer Herzog, Swiss Finance Minister, 1870

Chapter 16
37 *The Futurist,* 1-2/95, p.14–17

Chapter 17
38 *News From Israel,* 7/89

Chapter 18
39 *Midnight Call,* 5/95, p.24
40 *Reuters,* 12/29/93

Chapter 20
41 *Catholic Register,* 9/74